Advance Praise for *The Confluence*

"I read *The Confluence* with more than a trace of envy because so few of us have the gift of keeping lifelong friends from college. As the chapters went by, and I saw these friendships ripen and deepen, I realized the book goes beyond one college and one shared backwoods tract. It's about the very meaning of friendship and young people growing older together."

> — **MEL ALLEN**, *YANKEE MAGAZINE*

"Any longtime outdoorsman knows how marvelous sporting friendships can be... Any writer knows that he or she can never quite adequately express the profundities, but each of these essayists, so different one from the other and so emphatically akin, comes as close as any of us is likely to get. A bright and wonderful read!"

> — **SYDNEY LEA**, POET LAUREATE EMERITUS OF VERMONT

"This land at the summit of New Hampshire is large and wild and very special; so is its evocation in these pages. Instigators Odence and Van Wie and their merry band of friends. . .write well and, dare it be said, charmingly about their times together in the far American north. The memories differ (as memories do), and that's all to the good. The inspirations differ, too, from Corey Ford and Norman Maclean…to Moe, Larry and Curly. Van Wie is a fine photographer with a poetic eye, while Odence and Chamberlin are his equals in illustration. . . a constantly warm, regularly moving reflection."

> — **ROBERT SULLIVAN**, AUTHOR OF *FLIGHT OF THE REINDEER* AND *A CHILD'S CHRISTMAS IN NEW ENGLAND*

"*The Confluence* is a joyful read. . . It is the kind of book that makes us realize there is a lot more to fishing than fish."

> — **DANIEL W. GALHARDO**, TENKARA USA

"Camaraderie pervades *The Confluence*: warmth, humor, touches of pathos, a shared love of fish and flies, special waters, also art and literature… a collection of stories, essays and art compounded and distilled by seven literate friends. . . Steadily engaging, often surprising, the prose here is polished but blessedly unpretentious. . ."

> — **SETH NORMAN**, *FLY ROD & REEL*, ROBERT TRAVER AWARD WINNER, AND PULITZER PRIZE NOMINEE

"I wholeheartedly recommend this book to young and old."

— RALPH N. MANUEL, PhD, RETIRED DEAN OF DARTMOUTH COLLEGE

"*The Confluence*, which I read in one sitting, shows how this splendid remnant of the original New England wilderness, with its rugged mountains, big woods, icy rivers and tropically-colored brook trout, has shaped the outdoor experiences and nurtured the friendships of those who know and love it."

— HOWARD FRANK MOSHER, WINNER OF THE NEW ENGLAND INDEPENDENT BOOKSELLERS PRESIDENT'S AWARD

"After reading only the first few pages… I was swept downstream in the Diamond River and experienced the pleasures of the braided current of short essays by this group of Dartmouth friends… The book transcends the Dartmouth Grant and captures the essence of any annual pilgrimage by a group of dear friends to a secluded place. Nice work, Boys!"

— EVELYN KING, REGISTERED MAINE GUIDE, FFF CASTING INSTRUCTOR AND BOWDOIN ALUMNA

"Plan your evening wisely, *The Confluence* is a book that refuses to be put down. Sustaining friendships requires glue. With elegance, grace and good humor, the authors make a compelling case for fly fishing being one such form of glue. Space on my bookshelves is jealously guarded, but room will be made for *The Confluence*."

— GRAYDON HILYARD, AUTHOR OF *CARRIE STEVENS, MAKER OF RANGELEY FAVORITE TROUT AND SALMON FLIES*

"I can't say enough good about the thoroughly entertaining collections of stories that make up *The Confluence*. If you know in your soul that fishing with friends is one of the great joys of fishing and that the experience is enhanced by wild places, then don't miss the chance to add this book to your library."

— TOM SADLER, OUTDOOR WRITER, FLY-FISHING GUIDE, AND TENKARA AFICIONADO

"This is a wonderful book about fishing—and like all wonderful books about fishing, the fishing both matters and doesn't. . . It isn't a 'how-to-fish' book, rather it is a 'how-to-live' book."

— DAVID SCOTT KASTAN, GEORGE M. BODMAN PROFESSOR OF ENGLISH, YALE UNIVERSITY

"Robert Louis Stevenson said that as travelers in the wilderness of this world the best we can find in our travels is an honest friend, or, as the authors of *The Confluence* suggest, an honest group of friends. From my work with men and my research on their friendships, I was impressed with how drawn in I was... No doubt I'd been hooked."

    – **ROB GARFIELD, MD**, AUTHOR OF *BREAKING THE MALE CODE: UNLOCKING THE POWER OF FRIENDSHIP*

"To paraphrase Henry David Thoreau, many men go fishing all of their lives without knowing that it is not the fish they are after. This fine collection of stories created around memories spawned in the clear cold waters of a very special part of the great north woods, wonderfully illustrates the essence of what Thoreau's sentiments mean to all who truly appreciate their time on the water."

    – **BILL PIERCE**, OUTDOOR SPORTING HERITAGE MUSEUM, RANGELEY, MAINE

"*The Confluence* is appealing on many levels... Those who love fly fishing will love this book, but it is much more a moving story about great friendship over a lifetime."

    – **WILLIAM GOODSPEED**, AUTHOR OF *BUZZ KILL*

The Confluence

Fly-fishing & Friendship *in the* Dartmouth College Grant

I envy not him that eats
better meat than I do,
nor him that is richer,
or wears better clothes
than I do;
I envy nobody but him,
and him only,
that catches more fish
than I do.

Izaak Walton *The Compleat Angler*

Bob Chamberlin's eye for combining the beauty of the word with the craft of graphic design is shown in his hand-set letterpress print of this Izaak Walton quotation with his own drawing of a streamer fly.

The Confluence

Fly-fishing & Friendship *in the* Dartmouth College Grant

A Collection of Essays, Art, and Tall Tales

David Van Wie
Phil Odence
Norm Richter
Bob Chamberlin
Ed Baldrige
Dave Klinges
Bill Conway

Peter E. Randall Publisher
Portsmouth, New Hampshire
2016

First Printing: May 2016

Peter E. Randall Publisher
PO Box 4726
Portsmouth NH 03802

www.perpublisher.com

ISBN-10: 1942155123

ISBN-13: 978-1942155126

Library of Congress Control Number: 2016930046

www.confluencebook.com

All photographs in this book, including the front and back covers, are by David Van Wie unless otherwise noted.

Excerpt from *Mama Makes Up Her Mind: And Other Dangers of Southern Living* by Bailey White, copyright 2009. Reprinted by permission of Da Capo Press, a member of the Perseus Books Group.

Testament of A Fisherman by Robert Traver is reprinted by permission of Kitchie Hill, Inc.

Distributed by University Press of New England
www.upne.com

Contents

Dedication

First, we dedicate this book to our parents, who nurtured us with the values and interests reflected in this book, and who gave us the opportunity to attend Dartmouth College.

Second, we dedicate this to our families. What a fabulous Father's Day gift you all have given us year after year: time for our annual adventure in the North Country!

Third, we dedicate this to Dean Ralph Manuel. You welcomed us to Dartmouth and challenged us to make a "significant positive impact" in this world. You have continued as a mentor and role model, and we have your forty-plus years of visiting the Grant as inspiration to keep on keeping on.

Finally, we dedicate this to our Alma Mater, Dartmouth College, with our deepest appreciation for the special community you provided us and for the extraordinary places—like the Second College Grant, our source of renewal and wonder—that you shared with us. What a privilege it is to be a Dartmouth alum!

Acknowledgments

We would like to thank Cheryl Bascomb for her support and patient review of many drafts from beginning to end. Thanks, also, to Patricia Berry ('81) for her encouragement and keen eye in integrating the stories and editing our drafts.

We wish to share our deep appreciation of the team at Peter E. Randall Publisher for their guidance through the final editing and publishing process: Deidre Randall for taking on this unique group of authors in the first place; Grace Peirce for her fabulous work on book design; and Dale Kuhnert for insightful edits and candid feedback on the manuscript.

And finally, a special thanks to Jill Osgood for creating such a beautiful map of the Grant and the Confluence.

Foreword

When asked to write a foreword for this book, I immediately remembered my first visit to the Dartmouth Grant. My friend Dave Van Wie had invited me to a fly-fishing weekend with him and a bunch of his Dartmouth friends. I pretty much knew what to expect.

As a Cornell alum, I was going to have to put up with some good-natured ribbing and no doubt listen to endless Dartmouth stories. What fun. Still, I wanted to fish the Grant, and Dave was my longtime fishing partner.

I have been along on plenty of guys-only fishing weekends, and I know how they go. Lots of fishing, of course, and then, because this is usually a chance for hard-working and family-oriented guys to cut loose a little, plenty of drinking, cigar smoking, belching, farting, and off-color jokes and stories. The food can be either really good or really bad, but it is hard to predict. Of course, there isn't much bathing, shaving, or grooming—a broad-brimmed fishing hat with a splash of DEET covers up things nicely.

I arrived at the cabin after everyone else, but I knew that I was in the right place. The vehicles that were parked here clearly belonged to Dartmouth alums: SUVs or similar (but not the really big ones that are environmentally unfriendly), and several Dartmouth bumper stickers or vanity plates with some misspelling of the word *green*, like GREEEN. I am sure there is tough competition for the best GO GREEN plate.

I was soon to realize that this group was not the typical bunch of fly-fishing bums that I was familiar with. One guy was sitting on the cabin steps strumming a guitar; another was fiddling with the settings of his camera, trying to catch a photo of a hummingbird; and another had his watercolors out and was painting a landscape. The food was gourmet with choice wines and beers. These guys were getting the most out of their weekend at a rustic cabin.

As I watched their various activities and listened to them catch each other up on the twists and turns of their lives, I realized that this was not just a fishing trip. It was a more of a Renaissance-Men-Go-Fishing retreat—a Thoreauvian chance to commune with the outdoors, recharge the soul, pursue a favorite leisure activity, and commiserate about the travails of life with longtime friends. Of course, there was still plenty of drinking.

And there was plenty of fishing to be done. In my experience this can often get competitive, racing to the best spots and trying to outfish your friend for bragging rights. Sometimes fishing carnage ensues. Picture a pack of hyenas fighting over a carcass for the best scraps.

Not this group though. There were a few novice fly fishermen in the crew, so everybody was sharing knowledge and suggesting the best flies to use, with the more experienced guiding the others. It was more like a pack of overeducated wolves, hunting as a group and coordinating efforts, so overall success would be higher. And all the fish we caught were released to play another day.

That trip was remarkable, but reading through the stories that follow, I learned that each outing to the Grant has been remarkable in its own way. Some years were great victories with many nice fish landed, and other years were a struggle. The Dead Diamond and Swift Diamond rivers are free-wheeling freestone streams, susceptible to floods and droughts. Consequently, in the years when the weather doesn't cooperate, fishing can be tricky. But every trip is a success because, while fishing seems to be the main event, it is in fact just an excuse to reconnect, rekindle, and realize that, even with the challenges and difficulties we all must face, life can be really damn good.

Read a chapter or two of *The Confluence* when you have a free moment. You will certainly find a lot to like in this collection of stories and reflections, especially if you have a connection to Dartmouth, have visited the Dartmouth Grant, or just enjoy fly-fishing a favorite remote stream. Moreover, this book will resonate with anyone who appreciates the camaraderie that develops among good friends who get together year after year and, to their credit, decade after decade.

—Lou Zambello is the author of *Flyfishing Northern New England's Seasons* (Wilderness Adventures Press, 2014) and a columnist for *The Maine Sportsman*.

Introduction: At The Confluence

By David Van Wie

The note on the table in Sam's Cabin said:

> Fishing at the Confluence
>
> -P

I couldn't wait to get out and join them.

I had arrived at the Grant later than planned because I'd had to finish up some work in the office for the Project From Hell. A crazy rush to a client deadline often happens when you're planning to take time off. Clients are important, but not as important as my trip to the Grant. I wouldn't miss it for the world.

This year, 2006, made it thirteen years that we'd fished together in mid-June. My late start meant that I didn't make the usual rendezvous at noon at LL Cote in beautiful downtown Errol, New Hampshire. Norm and Phil had come and gone by the time I arrived at that eclectic outpost, purveyor of sporting goods and general merchandise. I picked up a few flies and my Granite State fishing license and headed up Route 16 toward the entry road. On their way in, my friends kindly had left the key in our usual hiding spot near the gate. It was only a mile or so from the entrance to our cabin.

I parked next to Phil's red Jeep and began unpacking the gear from my car so I could get to my fishing stuff and join them on the river. I put my fly-tying kit, watercolors, and guitar in the corner of the living room. There were sleeping bags in each of the two bunk rooms, so I tried to figure out which one would have less snoring. I threw my sleeping bag, pillow, and duffel bag onto the lower bunk in the room on the left. The mattresses aren't so great, but it looked like I would have one of the firmer mattresses. Phil had piled his stuff on the other bunk.

I opened my cooler to see what needed to go in the fridge. A propane-powered refrigerator is a curiosity in the twenty-first century, as are the gas light fixtures in every room of the cabin. But they are handy luxuries in a remote camp, miles from the nearest power line. I wasn't too surprised to see that the fridge was mostly full of beer already. Bob, who does the bulk of the food shopping, wasn't expected until later in the afternoon, so I stowed my assigned breakfast items and went out onto the porch to rig up my fly rods.

I like to carry two fly rods whenever I fish for trout: a 4-weight rod rigged with floating line and a dry fly, and a heavier 5- or 6-weight rod rigged with sinking line or sinking tip for wet flies or streamers. There is a loop and a Velcro latch on my fishing vest that allow me to attach the reserve rod to my chest upright like an antenna sticking out of my left shoulder, safely out of the way of my right-hand casting. This contrivance allows me to switch back and forth without wading to shore for my other rod. I often start fishing with a small streamer on the sinking line and then switch to the dry fly rig if I see a trout rise or a hatch starting.

I pulled on my waders and put on my vest bulging with fly boxes and tools. Trudging down the road, I crossed the bridge (looking for rises on the water below), and turned down the trail to the Confluence, where the Swift Diamond and Dead Diamond rivers join, just above the Diamond Gorge. "Where the Swift meets the Dead" sounds a bit like a cowboy movie, but no cowboy hats here. My blue Trout Unlimited cap and polarized sunglasses completed my outfit.

The river flow was favorable, and the sky was more clouds than sun. I stepped into the water at a place where you can look upstream in both rivers and reached down to feel that the water temperature was properly chilly. Phil, wearing the blue plaid shirt that Billy constantly gives him shit about (and which has recently come back in style), was fifty yards upstream fishing the pocket water on the Swift, among a few larger cascades that give way to some bouldery runs. He was wader-less, as is his preference, and knee deep in the gin-clear water. I could see Norm's trademark red cap downstream, near the head of the Gorge and knew that he was again on his never-ending quest for the legendary lunkers rumored to inhabit the top few pools before the Gorge becomes inaccessible.

The entrance to Diamond Gorge, rumored to be the home of legendary lunkers, is just below the Confluence.

I waded out to the tail of a deep pool next to a rock the size of a pickup truck and got a wave from Phil, but Norm was too intent on his efforts to notice me several hundred yards away. I started with my sinking tip line and a small version of a Wood Special streamer that I tied myself, nicknamed Dave's Woody by some wiseass—maybe me. On the fourth or fifth cast, as the streamer swung in a dancing jig across a large submerged rock, I felt the throb and wobble of a trout taking the fly. Moments later, after guiding the fish out of the faster current into the eddy below my feet, I landed my first wild brook trout of the trip. "No skunk for me," I muttered to myself.

This was bliss. There is no place else I would rather be than standing in the river with these guys here in the Dartmouth Grant.

After an hour of moving from pool to glide, I saw the dust from a car rumbling up the dirt road along the river. Norm had worked his way back upstream to me, lunker-less still but happy to have hooked two splendid brookies. We waved to Phil that we were heading back to greet Bob or Billy or Ed or Dave—whoever was just arriving.

Back at the cabin, there were broad smiles, eyes bright with the delight of reunion, good-natured insults, and hugs, which, over the years, have evolved from handshakes. We cracked open a few beers as the greetings continued and stories began. Then we all headed out onto the river until dusk and dinnertime. Another year, another adventure.

————

As their names suggest, the Swift Diamond River and Dead Diamond River have very different personalities. The Swift Diamond charges rapidly from west to east, with turbulent rapids and the occasional deeper moments in pools and glides amid rocks, boulders, and granite ledges. The Dead Diamond flows from north to south across more moderate terrain. Meandering stretches of slow water and calm runs are punctuated by deep pools behind rocky outcrops with poetic names like Slewgundy, Monahan's Bathtub, Sid Hayward Ledge, and the formidable Hellgate Gorge.

Downstream of where the two rivers join, at the Confluence, the Diamond River drops into the remote depth of Diamond Gorge, a quarter-mile-long gash in the low hills, and then enters a long straight charge into the outside world. The river's brief run through the gorge is largely hidden from view. A few outlooks from the ridge above allow the adventurous viewer a glimpse of the excitement below, but that's about it.

This cascade on the lower Swift Diamond River provides holding pools for many wild trout.

This book is about another confluence that occurs once a year in the Second College Grant, a 28,000-acre timber reserve owned by Dartmouth College in the northern tip of New Hampshire. This is the confluence of the lives of seven grown-up boys, graduate and undergraduate classmates at Dartmouth, who have been meeting to fish each June for almost twenty-five years.

For three days, we share close quarters in a remote cabin with few amenities. The main draw is the wilderness, and the precious opportunity to put aside phones, email, and the stresses of modern life to fly-fish for wild brook trout. It is also an opportunity for good friends to share our individual and mutual passions in life: conversation, cooking, beer, wine, art, politics, music, and then some. It is a chance to catch up on families, careers, hopes, and dreams before charging back into the outside world until the following June.

The idea for this book came about when Bob Chamberlin and I were fishing the Diamond River below the Gorge on the last day of our 2014 trip. My mind wandered while I was casting in the afternoon sun. My wife, Cheryl, had been encouraging me for years to write a book about the Grant, and I was thinking about how I would approach such a project. Reflecting on twenty-some years of Grant visits, I realized that our group—we call ourselves The Boys of the Grant or just The Boys—had numerous stories and memories that we revisited each year. It occurred to me that all of us are capable storytellers, so wouldn't it be cool if everyone contributed a story?

Each of the guys would have his own perspective on our various adventures, and we could include some of our original watercolors and photos. This would be a fun way of capturing the highlights of our weekends, not only for ourselves but also for our friends and families. It even crossed my mind that others—maybe folks with an interest in fly-fishing or Dartmouth or traditional gatherings with good friends— might enjoy our project. Plus, it would be an opportunity for each of us to reflect on what he has brought to and gained from our annual retreat.

I floated the idea past Bob as we stowed our waders to head home. He liked the idea and agreed to contribute. After thinking about it during my two-hour drive home that afternoon, I became convinced this would be a worthwhile endeavor. That evening, I sent an email to

The Boys explaining what I had in mind and asking them to contribute something—essays, photos, artwork, or vignettes—from their individual recollections and archives of our myriad adventures over the years. I would pull all the parts together and figure out what was next.

It took Dave Klinges all of six minutes to respond enthusiastically. "We have to include The Fallen Soldier story," he wrote, adding "Dibs!" Others chimed in with some ideas, a few smart-aleck comments, and at least mild commitment. I learned later that a few thought the idea would die on the vine like many well-intentioned projects. Philip asked rhetorically if perhaps we should wait for our fiftieth year.

But I couldn't drop the idea. I wrote a few pieces and sent some drafts and a prospective table of contents out to provide encouragement and food for thought. Two weeks later, Dave Klinges's "Fallen Soldier" draft arrived. He'd nailed it. I was impressed, and not a little relieved that I was no longer the only one providing momentum.

It was fascinating to see Dave's take on that story about an older fellow, disabled by Parkinson's, who scared the hell out of his buddies—and The Boys, who were called on to help—when he disappeared into the woods one day. It shouldn't have surprised me. Seven guys will remember an episode through seven filters. And as you might expect, all of our recollections are subject to the vagaries of time. A few episodes here are retold by different Boys, and the variations in our recollections have resulted in some interesting debates, as well as unearthing of old photos and cabin logbooks to nail down dates and details. It has been a hoot to read others' insights and reflections.

Phil, in particular, was hooked after writing a couple of stories and threw himself into the project. Initially, he thought the essays should be exclusively about fishing, and we tried to oblige. But it soon became clear that fishing was the *vehicle* for our journeys, not the journey itself. In the end, the stories were more about us, and less about the fish.

As the stories, essays, and even a tall tale (Norm likes to write fiction) came together, we realized we had assembled more than a collection of amusing accounts. The book as a whole not only provides glimpses into our lives, it also tells how we have grown and influenced each other as men, as fathers, and as friends. In a sense, you hold in your hands a confluence of our spirits, one that is in the context of our deep respect for the Grant and the sense of place it provides each of us.

Oh, and yes, there is still quite a bit of fishing.

In these pages, we will introduce you to many characters. You'll get to know The Boys, certainly, and also a dog or two, the Grant, its cabins, the fish we visit with, and our favorite places and activities. In some sense every road, every stream, and even a few rocks play parts in the story. You'll meet them all.

Dartmouth College is also a character throughout the book, as is our close-knit Class of 1979. Dartmouth has played a big part in our lives beyond these weekends. Two of The Boys married Dartmouth women, and several have offspring who attend or have graduated from the College on the Hill, as our Alma Mater is referred to. The Dartmouth Experience borders on cultish (or so non-Dartmouth spouses have said), but it's a good kind of cult. Our Grant adventures would not be possible if it were not for the special bonds that Dartmouth engenders. This book is our celebration of that legacy. With this writing we welcome the reader into the Dartmouth family.

We hope you will see that the whole is greater than the sum of the parts. And The Boys of the Grant look forward to writing the sequel to *The Confluence* for our fiftieth anniversary.

A Note About Names

A few of us have nicknames used throughout the book. I (Dave Van Wie) was nicknamed Guy (pronounced *ghee*) as a sophomore, so most of my friends from Dartmouth still call me Guy. With so many Davids in my generation, Guy was a handy moniker as I was the only one with it on campus. Bob, whom I met years later in grad school, never picked up the Guy habit, so he calls me Dave or DVW, as I typically sign my name. Because our stories are conversational, each author has written the names as he would speak them.

The other Dave (Dave Klinges) is almost universally called Klingon by all of us, including Bob. Hopefully, that will help keep the two Daves straight throughout the narrative.

The others have nicknames used occasionally in these stories but they should be easy to identify in context. Norm is sometimes Nerm. Billy is sometimes Young Conway. And Phil Odence's nickname in college was Dense, but we never call him that, because we know he is anything but.

A Note About The Dartmouth Grant

The Dartmouth Grant is open to the public for non-motorized use, including hiking, fishing, hunting, mountain biking, orienteering, snowshoeing and cross-country skiing. Camping and open fires are prohibited in the Grant. Use of the cabins in the Grant is limited to Dartmouth students, alumni and employees and their guests, as is access through the gates by motor vehicles. For more information, visit the Dartmouth Outdoor Programs website (http://outdoors.dartmouth.edu/services/cabins/).

Coming Together

By Phil Odence

I f you traced on a map each of our paths to the Grant, the drawing would appear much like a watershed. Everyone navigates his own tributary, flowing from the headwaters of our respective real worlds, skirting the Great Lakes and up the eastern seaboard, joining with others at points along the way and ultimately meandering into the Dartmouth College Grant.

———

Norm's and my paths, for instance, converge at Logan Airport. His German heritage brings to mind the word for airport, *Flughafen*, literally meaning Flight Harbor; I love that. I land at the curb outside baggage claim where Norm has claimed an enormous duffel and the long brown canvas-covered cylinder that contains his rod. He has packed the night before and thrown his stuff in his trunk, allowing him to head to O'Hare straight from work. He stows his gear in the Jeep, and we are off on an oxbow turn through my urban 'hood for drinks, dinner, and talk of careers and families and books and writing.

Norm "Nerm" Richter grew up in the Big Apple where his parents settled after immigrating from Europe after World War II. He arrived at Dartmouth in the autumn of '75, never having seen the campus or much else north of Connecticut, and became my roommate and first (and fast) Big Green friend. Nowadays he knows more about corporate taxes than anyone, having worked on Capitol Hill after law school writing tax laws before he headed off to help large corporations understand and comply with them. After marrying a gal from Block Island, he became a saltwater fisherman. He started his family a little later than the rest of us and thus still has pre-college-age daughters. As the father of two girls myself, I'm always happy to field his parenting questions.

1

I really appreciate the guys who come from afar. It costs each an extra day and an extra grand to join us, but Norm never missed a beat when he moved for work from Providence to Chicago. And it's a good thing, too, because the cabin banter would not be the same without his perspectives on literature, politics, and beer. We all depend on his Friday quesadillas and I especially depend on Nerm to laugh at all my jokes.

After dinner and drinks in my neighborhood, we get a good night's sleep and typically set off for the Grant early, ahead of the commuter traffic. As with any recreational sojourn, the anticipation-filled departure and journey are far more enjoyable than the paddle back upstream. "Half the fun is getting there," an old airline ad used to say, and these few hours in the Jeep pointed north are some of the best of my year.

I am ever struck by the steady gradient of civilization as one travels from Boston to the North Woods. Unlike entering the Boston Public Garden or Central Park, where passing through a stone gate transports one abruptly from urban craziness to pastoral splendor, the civilized world steadily, but only gradually, recedes from the landscape while we are en route to the Confluence.

The average Joe, on approaching Franconia Notch, feels like he is officially "out in it." For us, though, the Notch is less than two thirds of the way to our ultimate destination, north of the mountains. The last hints of the real world (and for me, most of its attendant stresses) continue to recede through that last third of the way.

Distracted by the dramatic peaks of the White Mountains, perhaps, one loses sight of the fact that the road through the Notch is still an interstate with lines and guardrails and signs directing travelers to scenic overlooks and visitor parking. But soon interstate turns to state highway; the signs get smaller and sparser; service stations get shabbier and lose national branding. Towns like Lancaster, Groveton and West Milan (that's *MY-lin*, for the unacquainted) become progressively less town-like.

Billy "Young" Conway is at Baltimore-Washington Airport now, awaiting the departure of Southwest Flight 360 to Manchester. His path will join with ours in a few hours. We'll probably be knee deep in the Swift Diamond River, purposefully in sight of the dirt road that roughly parallels the river and where he will ride into the picture in a mid-size rental car.

Billy, a consummate gentleman, hails from New Orleans originally, and he spent summers on Martha's Vineyard and many happy hours bluefishing. We met freshman fall on the soccer field at Dartmouth and shared the disappointment of not making the team. He ended up rowing lightweight crew while I played rugby. After our sophomore summer, I talked Young Conway out of doing volunteer work on an Indian reservation to instead spend three months on a Kerouac-like excursion across America. After graduation, like Norm, Billy attended law school and spent his early career on the Hill writing energy laws. Now Bill is a partner in the energy practice at Skadden Arps in D.C. Oh, and he lives in a haunted house with his wife, Diana, and the youngest of his three kids. The other two are in college.

What Billy brings to the party (literally) is the wine. His journey will wind through the New Hampshire State Liquor Store where he'll pick up the weekend's supply. A classic renaissance man, he is comfortable with backhoe, beehive, or soufflé dish. He also brings a delightful bent for stimulating conversation on almost any topic—and how nice for him that his own views are always correct. A trip would not be the same without Billy, although his absence would have no impact on the dishes getting washed.

The nickname "Young Conway" comes from a comic strip I created in college that was dedicated to laying all Billy's foibles bare and trampling on his ego. He was my biggest fan. We remain friends because he's incredibly gracious at suffering ridicule. Nerm and I smile thinking Bill's on his way.

———

As Norm and I meander north of the White Mountains, signs of modern human life continue to fade. The final stretch is Route 16, which parallels the west bank of the Androscoggin River. This waterway drains Umbagog Lake and winds across the border into Maine before joining with the Kennebec River at Merrymeeting Bay, ultimately feeding into the Gulf of Maine. By this point in the journey, we're not in Kansas anymore, Toto. The roadbed here is just a few feet above the marshy waters on either side, and although road signs pop up here and there, most warn of moose crossings and collisions. The lucky traveler may even spot a moose or two wallowing in a mud pit by the roadside.

––––––––

If Bob Chamberlin is on schedule, his journey will merge with ours shortly. While our drive may loop through Berlin, New Hampshire, Bob will pass Berlin, Vermont, on the west side of the state's Northeast Kingdom, as he wends his way from Burlington. In the passenger seat will likely be a mixed-breed canine. Once it was the faithful Bogie, first of our party to depart this earth for the Great Unknown; now it's Jack, a worthy successor.

Guy and I met Bob in grad school, a small, funky systems engineering program at Dartmouth's Thayer School. Bob's the only midwesterner of the bunch. He'd grown up in Illinois and attended the University of Wisconsin as an undergraduate. After grad school, he continued to reside in the Upper Valley of the Connecticut River, mostly in Norwich, Vermont. He's a transportation engineer and now runs his company's Burlington office, making us all jealous over his ability to walk to work. Bob, too, has a couple of great kids and is the only one of our bunch who has divorced. That said, the rest of us are all pretty baffled as to why our own wives have hung in as long as they have.

It's quite possible Bob will not be on schedule because he's Bob and because he does the food shopping. He took over from me as quartermaster fifteen years ago, and The Boys keep hoping that with experience he'll eventually figure it out. He may be standing in an aisle right now trying to remember the one thing I implored him not to forget.

So, yes, Bob brings dogs and food—and paints. Bob is a professional artist and produces watercolors that delight and receive actual critical acclaim. Oh, and he's about the nicest guy in the world, so never mind about the food-shopping skills.

––––––––

After several miles of sparse camps and mobile homes, the town of Errol emerges up ahead of Norm and me. No more than a crossroads really, it stands out as a metropolis against the natural backdrop. Errol features the Northern Exposure Restaurant (1.5 stars on Yelp), a couple of motels catering to hunters and snowmobilers, and Androscoggin Taxidermy. The jewel of the village is LL Cote, or more correctly the LL Cote Sport Center—not to be confused with and, to be clear, nothing like L.L. Bean.

Opened in 1986 as a fishing store in an old white farmhouse, it stood that way when we arrived on the scene twenty-some years ago. But in 2004, LL Cote's owners transformed it into a backwoods megastore, a cross between Walmart and Cabela's. At the entrance, the customer is greeted by an enormous stuffed albino moose flanked by a number of other stuffed creatures representing much of the local fauna, all no doubt the handiwork of Androscoggin Taxidermy.

With an enormous selection of flies and other fishing gear, LL Cote can certainly supply all your angling needs. As I recall, when we first visited, the inventory of the place was mostly centered on fishing and hunting, but today the 30,000-square-foot monster store caters to a much wider range of interests and has become a bustling center of activity for Coos County, the northern panhandle of New Hampshire.

We spend most of our time in the fishing room, which thankfully has changed very little since our early days. The fly counter probably has more choices today and many new gadgets. Leaders and fly-tying gear cover the walls.

Only a couple of times have I ventured all the way up into the gun department. The vast array of weapons and ammo is staggering. Archery, too, is big, with those crazy-looking high-tech bows that bear scant resemblance to what they gave us, albeit misguidedly, back in gym class. Pretty much any way you want to kill an animal, LL Cote can provide the finest implements for doing so.

Their camping gear runs the way of Coleman. They will set you up with all the comforts of home to load into the shell-covered backend of your pick'emup truck, but you will find nothing high tech in this department, no ultralight camping gear for your Type A peak-bagger.

Similarly, the footwear section stocks mostly Sorel and Red Wing work boots, certainly nothing from Asolo or even Merrell that would serve you well on the Appalachian Trail. And the apparel at LL Cote tends towards camo, plus lots of woolens, flannel shirts, cargo pants, snowmobiling jumpsuits—pretty much everything a snappy-dressing outdoorsman could desire. Even, incredibly, a huge selection of camo lingerie and loungewear for the ladies to really warm up the cabin when winter rolls in.

The inventory goes on and on: dog crates, snowmobiles and ATVs, chainsaws, ear plugs, tractors, canoes, trailers, all manner of hardware, heavy-duty safes, candy bars, Weber grill knockoffs, sunscreen, toys, pots and pans, groceries, beer(!), bass boats, binoculars, snow shovels, bird feeders, over-the-counter medicines, plumbing supplies, picnic tables . . . and fishing licenses. That last item is the main attraction for us.

LL Cote is the most obvious meeting place for The Boys, especially now that it also has multiple lunch options in-store. We stop there every year. It's always late morning when Norm and I arrive, and we beeline for the fishing gear. The licensing process is a little slow—it still involves dictating name, rank, and serial number to be handwritten by the issuer and paid for in cash—so usually one of us starts that process while the other selects flies. Here's a tip: At the end of your annual trip or the season, jot down what flies you need for next year. Type it right into your iPhone. If I followed my own advice, I would save money, time, and consternation and wouldn't have so many of this one and a scarcity of that one.

Guy may be leaning up against his Subaru Outback wagon (fourth or fifth generation) as we land at LL Cote, or he may already be wandering around in the fishing section. He's able to time his arrival pretty accurately, as his branch of the stream is the shortest, originating in New Gloucester, Maine, a half hour north of Portland. He doesn't experience the dramatic contrast we all see coming from cities. New Gloucester is certainly a notch or two up from Errol, but it's still a far cry from the urban craziness most of us experience daily.

David "Guy" Van Wie grew up in Troy, New York. Like Billy's dad, his was a Dartmouth alum, and David spent many weekends in Hanover as a kid enjoying football games and reunions, before showing up two doors down from Norm and me in Cohen Hall freshman fall. An upperclassman nicknamed him Guy (pronounced *ghee*) because he thought "Guy Van Wie, French race car driver" suited David. The name stuck and Dartmouth friends use it to this day. An outdoorsman all his life, Guy is an environmental consultant and the only one of us to have served as an elected official, with a term in the Maine House of Representatives. His Dartmouth-graduate wife and kids were very supportive. In fact daughter Rosa later ran for his House seat, although she suffered the fate of most Democrats in that district.

If The Boys were a company, I suppose I'd be CEO and CFO and he'd be co-founder and COO or CTO. Anyway, The Boys will dispute just about anything, but there's no arguing that Guy is the best fisherman of the group by virtually any measurement. We've all been fishing for a long time, but Guy, well, he just does it better. He's also a font of knowledge about everything to do with the outdoors. Thankfully, he's a great teacher, too, and has made a fisherman of every one of us. He also brings the breakfasts for our weekend, so in the unlikely event that Bob forgets everything—it's not yet happened—we will at least have breakfast (the most important meal of the day) and wine. Lastly, I should mention that it was Guy who had the preposterous idea of writing this all down in a book.

———

After getting all our fishing needs squared away, we three trek the eighty yards to the other end of the store, which is set up like a convenience mart and includes a Subway counter. For the last five years I've had a twelve-inch hot Italian on flatbread with chipotle mayo. I have never eaten this sandwich anywhere else—don't even really patronize Subway—but there, on that first day of our annual outing, that's what I have. Every year.

We pay for our sandwiches plus a large bag of Lay's potato chips and a twelve-pack of craft ale and head out to the picnic table in front by the parking lot. I rarely indulge in potato chips, but what the hell. I frequently indulge in craft ales, but they somehow never taste as good as they do at the picnic table in front of LL Cote, washing down that hot Italian on flatbread while we watch the bustle of sportsmen, loggers, and bikers headed to Laconia and speculate about the arrivals of the rest of our group.

———

It's happened more than once that *just* as we are ready to set out for the last bend towards the Grant, someone else shows up and, goddammit, we are forced to pop open another Long Trail Ale. We forgive Ed for this inconvenience because he has come all the way from Kutztown, Pennsylvania, in his aircraft-carrier-sized SUV.

Ed Baldrige is a Pennsylvania native who arrived at Dartmouth from Allentown. He played rugby with Guy, Dave Klinges, and me, and knew the others of our band, though he was not particularly close with any of us while at school.

After graduating, through a series of fortuitous circumstances, Ed ended up trading on the Chicago Board of Trade and the Commodity Exchange in New York and, despite not knowing what the hell he was doing, was very successful and sharp enough to get out while he was ahead. Now he runs a wealth-management firm managing people's money in less risky investments. He, too, is an empty nester along with his wife, Lydia Panas, a stunning and acclaimed portrait photographer.

Ed joined the gang late, and we're still trying to figure out how he did it. We are at maximum capacity so it is difficult to deal with interest from other close, mutual friends. Maybe we will loosen up a bit when some of us start to kick off. But this club has no constitution and only unwritten rules. One of those rules, however, is that if a friend shows up from the cabin next door looking lost, you don't leave him out in the cold. And what a great fit Ed has been, bringing with him the fairly arcane concept of tenkara fishing, as well as advice on nymphing and investments ("stick it in a balanced indexed portfolio and leave it there; you will beat the 'pros' every time").

––––––––

Eventually the growing squadron shoves off down Route 16, which continues north. South of Errol it's called the Berlin (*BER-len*) Road, but becomes the Dam Road going north. It departs from the Andro-scoggin River just above Errol Dam and eventually picks up the Magalloway River, which flows into Umbagog Lake in such a screwy way that I can never figure out whether I am looking at the river or the lake as we drive along. The road gets a little narrower and consider-ably more pot-holed. Signs disappear altogether and the centerline's not been painted in recent years. The occasional camps and houses we've been passing become less occasional. After about five miles, the road bends a little east towards the border and Wilson's Mills, Maine. Just before the Maine border, we find ourselves in the town of Wentworth's Location. Don't blink.

If Errol is a crossroads, Wentworth's Location isn't. It's just a road with nothing intersecting it. About fifty people call the village home, and it boasts the Mt. Dustan Country Store & Cabins. The store is in a rickety-looking Victorian house with black shutters and a million signs, some handmade, out front, and it provides an eclectic range of supplies and convenience items, plus fishing licenses and a few flies. There's also a 1950s-era motel on the property. The store does too little business to justify keeping the doors open at all hours, but a knock or a ring brings a proprietor to the door, and she's invariably pleased to see you. As it's the final outpost, we have picked up a few items here when we've forgotten to procure something back in the "big city" of Errol.

––––––––––

Klingon may be on the way or he may not be. Despite all the planning, our trip often overlaps with the biannual Klinges family reunion. Most years he makes it, though, and when he does, like Billy he too meanders through Manchester Airport and grabs a rental car, one year a white Mustang convertible. Somehow, he and Billy can never coordinate schedules. Klingon's headwaters are in Princeton, New Jersey, right near the campus, and he hosts a mini-reunion whenever Dartmouth football is playing the Tigers in his neck of the woods.

David Klinges showed up in Hanover from Bethlehem, Pennsylvania, and did a brief stint as "Country Dave" due to his habit of pickin' and croonin' for the girls. But soon Klinges inevitably became "Klingon" and the world never looked back. He was an intense, fearless rugger and only recently gave up playing when yet another of his joints stopped working and required surgery. After graduating from Tuck School of Business, Klingon went the New York investment-banking route and is an expert at funding public infrastructure projects. He once told me unabashedly, "I've always liked finance because you don't have to work very hard, and they pay you a lot of money." He found a Dartmouth alumna who puts up with him and they too have great kids, one still studying in Hanover.

Klingon is the least likely of the bunch to spend three days in the woods or, say, anywhere else they don't deliver *The New York Times* to your door. It pains him to be out of touch with the Yankees and away from loud music. He's the most frustrated fisherman of the bunch, and there was a point when we thought he might not come back the next year, but he did and still does, and we're glad. He brings good whiskey, and he acts as a counterbalance to the group at times. When conversation wanders too far to the esoteric, Klingon shakes his head and picks up last week's copy of *Sports Illustrated*.

––––––––

Well beyond known civilization, a few hundred yards before the state line on the north side of Dam Road is a tidy little cemetery with about forty graves. Over a third of the inhabitants, if that's the right word, are Flints. There must be some history there, though I don't know it. Bounding the west side of the landmark Wentworth's Location Cemetery is the Dead Diamond Road, which runs north all the way through the Grant to Hellgate Gorge and beyond. Until this point, the roads have been paved, and so the dirt surface of the Dead Diamond Road demarcates the true end of the civilization that has been diminishing for roughly the last 200 miles. Across the dirt road from the cemetery is the little ranch-style house formerly occupied by Nelson Ham, longtime caretaker of the Grant. He had a classic, "can't get there from here" sense of humor and was noted for three signature jokes, or tall tales really, only one of which we remember. Here it is, in more or less Nelson's words:

A New Hampshire farmer was showing a flatlander from Boston the amazing pig that helped him pick apples every fall. The farmer would hold the pig up over his head to pick apples off of the tree and then set the pig down on the ground. With the apple still in its mouth, it would scamper over and drop it neatly into a basket.

The flatlander watched for a while and then remarked, "That is truly an amazing pig! But why," he wondered, "don't you climb up and shake the branches, and let your pig gather them up into the basket, rather than lifting him up to pick the apples one by one? Wouldn't that save time?"

To which the farmer responded, "Time? Why, time don't mean *nothin'* to a pig!"

Somehow, we find a way to use that punch line every year.

———

A half-mile up the road into the Grant is the gate, a horizontal arm of tubular steel that crosses the road between two stout posts. I'm usually driving, but when I can, I like to open the gate myself and let Norm pull the Jeep in. The gate has a heavy-duty padlock hanging through a thick metal tab that fits inside the post at one end. It's unlocked through a port in the side of the post. After unlocking the padlock with the key that arrived in the mail a week ago comes the fun part: bending over the gate at the waist and swinging across the road on it, then using it to sail back across after the car has gone through.

I grew up (though never to the point of eschewing a good gate swing) in southern New Jersey, and enjoyed summers sailing and fishing on Cape Cod where my father also spent his youth and met my mother. Mostly I've lived in New England since heading to Dartmouth and meeting The Boys (though I screwed around in Europe, Colorado, and California for a couple of years after grad school). I studied rugby, beer, and engineering and now work on the business side of technology

Phil turns the wheel over to Norm so he can enjoy his annual swing on the gate; thumbs up for another great trip!

companies. At the office, I'm known for running barefoot and for having climbed two 4,000-foot peaks in one day, wearing golf shoes. I was the first of The Boys to downsize, in our case from a farmhouse in Lincoln, Massachusetts. Having raised and shed two daughters, my wife, Beth, and I now reside between urban Waltham and Cotuit on Cape Cod.

But up in the North Country of New Hampshire, I'm the co-leader of Grant Troop 1979 and serve to keep us all physically strong, mentally acute, and morally straight.

————

Meanwhile back at the gate: the mosquitos are always a bitch this time of year, but even so we take a moment to peruse the entry signboard for updates to the usual notices about rock snot (or *Didymosphenia geminate*, a non-native algae that you don't want in your trout stream), studies-in-progress on the trout population, recommended catch limits, fishing restrictions, and other such news.

Soon after I ride the gate back across the road and we've locked out the real world, we drive by a large marsh on the left. Sadly, the towering dead tree (Guy would call it a snag) in the center of the marsh, that for so many years supported an active osprey nest, has fallen. The ospreys have rebuilt but the nest is no longer in the perfect spot to greet us upon arrival.

Down the road a bit are the old gatehouse and then the Perley Churchill Bridge. We just call it the Bridge. There's also a bridge north of Hellgate Gorge, which we also call the Bridge. Which is which is usually clear in context. Almost always we stop mid-bridge to survey the view up and down the river. This is our first definitive read on the height and speed of the water. "Looks a little low this year," we might say. We've never done particularly well downstream, but just upstream of the Bridge, we've caught some of the biggest trout we've seen in the Grant. A trip rarely goes by without our spending at least one early evening fishing upstream of the Bridge as far as the mouth of Diamond Gorge.

This osprey nest near the entrance to the Dartmouth Grant blew down in a winter storm and was rebuilt nearby the next spring.

We generally wear seatbelts in the Grant, as it's always possible that one might suddenly encounter a logging truck on the twisty one-lane roads. And once we came upon two poor bastards who had rolled their SUV into a ditch, maybe because they hit a bump or swerved to miss a deer. They didn't want to talk about it. But we don't think twice about drinking beer on the dirt roads of the Grant. Kids, don't try this at home, and I should make it clear, we don't drive impaired even in the Grant. I'm just talking about quenching a thirst on the way back to the cabin after a few hours of fishing. When we ultimately head back to civilization, we have to watch ourselves. More than once we've gotten as far as Route 16 just north of Errol before we realized that it was time to put the beers away.

A couple of miles north of the Bridge is the city center of the Grant, where the Swift Diamond Road peels off to the left between Sam's Cabin and the Management Center. One of these structures is usually our destination. Both are situated a short walk from the rivers' confluence. It may take a few hours, but soon The Boys will all have arrived.

The Origin

By Phil Odence

Whose idea it was to get me a fly rod one Christmas I don't know. Maybe it was my own idea. Maybe Santa Claus's. Most likely it was my wife, Beth's. Unlike me, she's good at filing away gift ideas during the year.

The previous spring, my father-in-law, Ted Tanner, had loaned me his nine-foot bamboo rod for the afternoon. It was an antique Heddon De Luxe that he had acquired before heading off to serve in Belgium during WWII. On the bank of a tributary to Alder Creek, west of the Adirondacks, he'd given me a little instruction on streamer fishing for brown trout. Evidently this was the first time any other human being had touched Ted's meticulously cared for rod. It registered with Beth that despite my getting nary a strike, I had enjoyed my first experience with fly-fishing. (Regina Tanner must have noticed as well, because after her husband died, about six years later, she presented me with the rod and various other prized items, including a leather wallet with about two-dozen old-school bucktail streamers.)

So, after Santa made his delivery, I was set up with a basic Orvis 6-weight and most of what I needed to get started. Oddly, it wasn't until a few years later that I finally procured a vest, but I didn't have a lot of stuff starting out. Between a pocket in the bib of my waders and a little Crown Royal bag I hung onto a buckle, I was able to cart along a small box of flies and a few other necessities. As these things go, you could probably still find a fly or two from that first batch in my current collection, this many years later.

Like most common folk, I assumed it was all about the cast. In retrospect, I guess it is true that you need to get casting out of the way before you can discover the multitude of other mysteries that come along in a lifetime of fly-fishing. Between the Orvis book she included and the gift certificate for lessons, Beth had taken care of the casting, too.

I started out practicing my casts in the backyard of 128 Reed Street, Lexington, Massachusetts, the house we moved into just a few weeks before our nuptials. I'd read somewhere that you are supposed to tie a little piece of fabric or some yarn on the end of the fly line—for visibility, I supposed. I'd carefully placed a trashcan lid in the snow as a target about twenty yards out from where I stood. There wasn't a lot more yardage than that in my little yard, especially when you account for the backcast, which initially I hadn't. Out of the box, I hung up the line in the pear tree that matched the painting Billy gave us as a wedding gift. I dug the iced-over wooden ladder out of the snow behind the barn and managed to free the line. But I didn't flip and flop too long before heading in to review the pictures in the book.

Come spring thaw, the lessons at Orvis in Wayland were helpful. The open shore of Lake Cochituate brought to mind the casting pools next to the polo field in Golden Gate Park I'd run past many times long ago during my "year of living impulsively." Even then I'd been intrigued by the old guys out on a Tuesday morning, casting back and forth with that graceful motion and what I now know as tight loops. Since my Orvis instructor would take two for the price of one, Beth came along for lessons as well, and it quickly became apparent that *"She could'a' been a contenda!"* Actually, we both did okay, and after a couple of hours felt ready to slay the wiliest of trout.

————

It was during the summer of 1992 that I landed my first beast, one of many highlights that wonderful summer. In June, Beth and I had made the decision to migrate to Hanover, and it worked out that I was not to start my job at High Performance Systems there until mid-September. I was off for nearly three glorious months. The kids were almost two and four, and we were living on the Cape. One fine afternoon, I packed up rod, tackle, waders, beers, wife, and kids and drove a few miles down Quinaquisset Avenue to the headwaters of the Mashpee River.

A hundred years ago there was fine trout fishing in the Ice Age-created streams of the Upper Cape. Sea-run brook trout, or salters, were sport fished in coastal streams all along the New England coast.

Eventually, cranberry farmers on the Cape cleared away many of the trees that shaded these streams and channeled the water to irrigate bogs. All that added up to trout being subtracted from the Cape's list of sport fish. For the last three decades Cape Cod Trout Unlimited has been working to bring back the population, their efforts focused on the Quashnet River, the headwaters of which are just a couple of miles west of the Mashpee.

The river where I embarked didn't look a lot like the pictures in the Orvis books. (One day I would learn that there were sources other than Orvis for fly-fishing equipment and knowledge.) The river I chose was kind of overhung, the water was slow, and there were no rocks jutting upward or cut banks that the diagrams had indicated were sure places for fat trout to lurk. It was just water flowing between winding banks that didn't allow a lot of visibility.

My gang on shore erupted with high-pitched cheers after I'd slid in up to my waist and flipped a nameless dry fly out into the light flow. It was my first real cast, about a twenty-foot roll cast, as there was not a lot of room for airborne line in any direction. One, two, three, four . . . the fly couldn't have sat five seconds before it was struck like a gong by a ten-inch brook trout.

Not really. Actually it sat there undisturbed for considerably more than five seconds. And no fish.

The fly just sat there on the water, and I just watched it. After a while I concluded that it may not have been the best spot for a fish after all. "No, not yet girls; maybe next cast!" I called to my peanut gallery. I tried one over there. Then over there. And then another. I had my first taste of that multi-dimensional, never-solved fly-fishing conundrum: is it the fly pattern, color, size, drift, retrieve, location, depth? Or is it just that there are no fish? Or am I the worst fisherman on the planet? Probably some of all of the above.

It turned out there were fish, or, more accurately, there was a fish. My first on a fly. He was about five inches long, and I got him about twenty minutes later while changing positions and dragging the fly behind me, a technique many of us have since found surprisingly and, in a way, insultingly productive. But a fish is a fish.

My first small success that summer day in the Mashpee River inspired me to keep going for a while, but the kids were soon ready to retreat. And so ended my first fly-fishing expedition before the Grant trips.

––––––––

It was a fall football weekend in my new hometown of Hanover when I bumped into Bill Burgess, Dartmouth Class of '81 and a friend from Cotuit. The story of my stunning success on the Mashpee River captured his interest, and out of that discussion emerged the idea of a trip to Dartmouth's Second College Grant. Soon thereafter, I must have called Guy, the only fly fisherman I knew. He was game, of course, and thus was born our first June trip.

And so it was that one fine evening the following June, Burgess arrived at 6 Ledyard Lane, Hanover, in time for a late dinner. In addition to his duffel and sleeping bag, he was laden with a panoply of recent purchases. One day he too would learn about the world beyond Orvis, but not that day. Every one of those packages sported an Orvis logo. Owning exactly zero fly equipment when he awoke that morning, he'd left his desk in the mid-afternoon and beelined it to the downtown Boston Orvis store. Forty minutes later, Bill told me, he emerged from the store fully outfitted, with an additional $1,000 charge on his American Express Card. Tossing bags and boxes into the back of his Jeep Cherokee, he headed directly to Hanover.

We had fun after dinner, winding fly line backing onto a virgin reel, sorting and re-sorting flies into shiny new boxes, and drinking all my beers. The timetable and logistics formulated for our inaugural departure have altered little over decades of Grant excursions: late to bed, early to rise, and then straight to the LL Cote store in Errol for whatever items we have forgotten, plus our New Hampshire fishing licenses. It may also have been on that first trip that we worked out the double-secret key-hiding spot and initiated many of the other traditions that stand today.

Burgess and I entered the Grant alone, ahead of Guy who was to arrive the next morning, and he ahead of his brother Doug and Burgie's friend Mark "Hubie" Heuberger. Which is how, on that first day, Burgess and I came to be the proverbial blind leading the blind. Once situated in Merrill Brook Cabin, we laid out the topo map of the Grant on the table in order to locate the river. We drove around much of the afternoon, scouting our options. Here and there we tried wading in a little, and I recall passing along some of my Orvis learnings. Our first real fishing was at the placid pools of Slewgundy late that afternoon.

Slewgundy. I will never be able to hear, read, think, or say the name without singing it in my head to the tune of "Moon River," as in "wider than a mile." *Sloooooo-gun-deeeee!* And, it was probably the name that attracted us to the spot. The water was fairly high, but we were able to get ourselves out across the jutting rocks that divide the upstream pools from the big one downstream. There's little room for more than two fishermen at Slewgundy. The best spots to fish from are atop the rocks separating the pools. When the water is low enough to get across on those rocks, one person can fish on one side and the other on the far side. We have since learned that an additional person or two can work their way around to the glide above the upper pools. But on that night, it was just Bill and Phil perched between the large, slow stretches of water.

For quite a while there was little activity. It was a bit reminiscent of my Mashpee River outing: water, flies, no idea what was going on underneath, and only a vague idea of what was going on above. How about here? How about there? But it was all good. Very good, in fact. We were out well beyond civilization, in real fish country, two guys, no kids, and a bunch of beers. Everything we could ask for to keep us in the game long enough for The Hatch.

I'd read about what a hatch looks like, and this was clearly one for the books. The memory may have been embellished a bit, but I am completely confident that, should we encounter a similar hatch today, it would cause each and every one of us to piddle our waders. And we'd certainly be better equipped to capitalize on it than Bill and I were that long-ago night, which is the point of the story.

It was an amazing sight. Suddenly the air was rich with hundreds and soon thousands of insects rising off the water, as they emerged en masse from below, transforming from nymphs to adults for their next life stage. It was as if a bomb had gone off under the fly counter at LL Cote. And then there were the rises. We noticed one here, one there, all frustratingly outside the range of our awkward casting. But soon expanding circles of water were everywhere as trout slurped and splashed and devoured the helpless bugs as they emerged from below and were poised momentarily on the surface of the water waiting for their wings to dry before taking flight.

It was more than a little heartening all of a sudden to have a target to aim for. And it didn't matter if you were off because there would be another rise near where your fly ended up anyway. Cast to one rise forward and there'd be three behind. There was no such thing as a back-cast; you could just flip directly from the pool in front of you to the one behind.

It was like shooting fish in a barrel—for someone with really bad aim and a really big barrel. Guy remembers that we caught something. I'm not so sure, but Burgess is quite certain we didn't (and he's now a Dartmouth Trustee, so we have to trust him). Maybe we had lied to Guy, rounded up, as it were. That would explain his memory. In any case, we certainly did not cash in on this epic opportunity.

It didn't matter. Burgess and I loved this fly-fishing thing. Looking back, that moment reminds me of a golf outing with Gerry Henderson, a sage old friend of my dad's, one summer during college. Off the tee on a long par 4, I accidentally drove one about 250 yards down the middle with perfect trajectory. As I looked up, I must have had a grin wider than the fairway. Gerry read my mind as he shook his head and said, "You think it's going to be like that every time now, don't you?" I did, and that's just how we felt that night at Slewgundy.

We had discovered fly-fishing. It was going to be like this every time. Bugs galore, rises everywhere, catching fish, and drinking beer. With respect to the beer at least, we were pretty accurate. But in twenty-plus years, The Boys and I have yet to see another hatch anything like that first evening at the Grant.

Settling In

By Phil Odence

Our annual excursion settled in to a marvelous consistency. The crew evolved over the years, but now The Boys of the Grant and our routines are well-established. December brings an email discussion of dates and cabin choice, though there's rarely much debate. Without ever meaning to, we seem to always pick Father's Day weekend. In April, I send out a headcount email that triggers a little back and forth with obligatory trash talking about Veg-All and my fishing wardrobe.

We shoot for LL Cote at noon on Thursday. We stash the gate key for the next ones to arrive. We talk, we fish, we cook, we paint. We bitch about who was snoring. Guy is Mr. Breakfast. Bob typically screws up some aspect of shopping, but we still have chicken on Friday and quesadillas Saturday. We stick Guy with cleanup on Sunday. That's the trip in a nutshell.

The big difference between the early days and more recent years is our daily routine. Our younger and more nimble constitutions were remarkably effective at shifting from a twenty-four-hour to a twelve-hour cycle. And we drank a lot more. Here's how it went:

We'd rise at 5:00 a.m., hungover. Eat a snack. Drink a beer while gearing up. Drive to our fishing spot and drink another beer. Fish for four hours while drinking beers. Motor back to the cabin. Cook something while drinking more beers. Eat around 10:00, and then engage in some form of recreation while drinking beers. I recall a drunken game of see-how-long-we-can-keep-the-badminton-birdie-in-the-air with some great diving saves.

We'd pass out around 1:00 p.m. After that all you have to do is change "a.m." to "p.m.," rinse, and repeat. That's pretty much the way we rolled in those days. We would have been perfectly adapted to settle a fishing planet that rotated every twelve hours. We were in our early thirties.

By years eight to ten, the routine had evolved. We certainly weren't downing a six-pack before lunch any more, and the sun was often up long before we were out of bed. Bill Burgess was no longer among us, although to this day he fishes as a member of a private club in northern Maine. Our crew had settled into more or less its current composition, although rare unavoidable conflicts sometimes kept one or two of us away. Habits and patterns and traditions had become established— certainly by year ten we were eating quesadillas for lunch and painting in the afternoons. The biggest difference between then and now is that I was still doing the shopping, so we had yet to start complaining about Bob's choices of food and beer.

We also drink more wine now. We fish until we're ready for a break but don't feel as driven to maximize fishing and beer consumption. Like the new Beaujolais, the early days were fresh and exciting, anticipated and satisfying. Time has smoothed the rough edges and blended the notes, and the vintage has mellowed into a familiar old favorite.

It is perhaps surprising that we've never taken this show on the road. There are, of course, countless places in the world that offer tremendous fishing, and now and then we talk about planning a trip to some famous or exotic fishing locale like Patagonia, Montana, or Labrador. But the farthest we've gotten is an occasional stop at the Androscoggin near Errol, and, one year when there were just no fish, we headed to a fishing camp over in Maine for a day. The reality is we all ration our vacation time. And I suspect not one of us would feel right breaking the rhythm. I imagine some year, probably when we are retired, we will augment our time together by adding another getaway, but I don't expect we will ever skip a year at the Grant. Why would we?

An Eddy in Time

By David Van Wie

Driving into the Grant is like turning back the clock. The dirt roads tunnel through the trees. I love that there are no power lines slicing at the canopy. The narrow, twisting lane demands a keen eye for moose, deer, or bears at every turn.

The few sparsely scattered cabins are built from huge peeled spruce logs—real logs, bringing to mind stories of Abe Lincoln and settlers pushing west. The gaslights, wood stoves, and banging wooden screen doors recall bygone eras. From the first, I relished the Grant's timelessness and was fascinated by its history, from ancient time when native peoples inhabited this area to the days of log drives and the camps that supported them.

When I visit a city, I often try to imagine what the landscape was like before cars and paved roads and tall buildings. What was the Meadowlands like when it was a meadow? What about Wall Street, quite literally a wall separating the Dutch colonists (including a Van Wie or two) in New Amsterdam from the wilderness of Manhattan Island? What kind of rural Massachusetts landscape did Paul Revere pass through during his famous ride? Across America, and especially the Northeast, growing cities, towns, and highways have replaced the wild landscape, as well as our agricultural and rural heritage.

But at the Grant, the opposite is true. I marvel at how the forest has reclaimed the land that was once occupied by logging camps and clear-cuts, and how time and the trees have wiped away most of the impact on the landscape. Not that long ago, a hundred or more men and a few women made the Grant their home in rough cabins, earning their living by cutting timber for the mills far downstream. Few visitors would suspect that the area around Hellgate was once a bustling village. Today, the Grant is essentially wilderness again.

A few years back, our classmate Rick Reno shared a book by Jack Noon, Dartmouth Class of '68, that explores the Grant's rich history. *Wintering with Amasa Ward 1889-1890* describes the camps and log drives that were in the Grant from the late 1800s until the early 1960s. Noon provides an engaging view into the effects of logging, past and present, on the rivers and ecosystems in the area, and his book gives regular visitors to the Grant something to think about and look for on every trip.

Merrill Brook Cabin, where Phil and I stayed on our first visit, is just down the road from the site of the old Upper College Farm. The Lower Farm was near the Gate Camp and the first bridge. All that is left of the farms now are a few fields that the caretakers mow once a year to clear openings for wildlife. I wish I knew what the farmers produced up here during the short growing season to feed the hungry men in the logging camps. Probably potatoes, cabbage, beans, squash, and apples. They also had to supply hay for dozens of draft horses, probably some oxen, and a few cows. On the Swift River Road, Phil once found a fat, rusty horseshoe the size of a pie plate.

The first time we fished at the head of Hellgate Gorge, Phil and I came across what we later confirmed were the remains of an old dam, with cables still bolted into the rock. Until the 1940s or 50s, the dam served to hold back the logs and water until the logging foreman was ready to release and run them all down to the mills on the Androscoggin River. There are photos in the Management Center showing men with long poles and pulp hooks breaking up a logjam near Four-mile Brook, several miles upstream along the Swift Diamond. From the pictures, it looks like treacherous work. It's easy to see how men must have died on these rivers while trying to make a living.

On our third trip to the Grant, our growing group (we had not yet begun to identify ourselves as The Boys) stayed up near Hellgate Gorge in the old Fish & Game Cabin, built in the early 1900s. The cabin and its attached bunkhouse were in sad disrepair, and mosquitoes swarmed in through the gaps in the logs and tormented us all night. As my brother, Doug, and I lay on top of our sleeping bags (it was too hot to be *in* them) swatting and cursing, we wondered aloud how the old-timers could have put up with the mosquitoes, black flies, and no-see-ums before the invention of Deep Woods OFF. These days I take a top sheet with me to the Grant to keep the most persistent bugs at bay on hot nights.

Fortunately, the Fish & Game Cabin was reconstructed in 2002. They jacked up the log structure, replaced the sills and floor, and moved the whole thing back across the field. It is now as comfortable as any other cabin in the Grant, which is to say still pretty darned rustic with the occasional mouse raiding your food, but that is part of the charm. The cabin was renamed in honor of Pete Blodgett, Class of '25, who first visited the cabin in 1922. Pete was a regular visitor to the Grant for many decades, and surely saw many changes in the landscape over his years.

A lesser known part of the Grant's history is the Native American people who lived in the Diamond River watershed and surrounding areas. When I walk the footpaths along the rivers, I sometimes picture how these same trails may have been used by Native Americans traveling through the valley. I am sure some were, but again, much of the landscape and vegetation, and even parts of the river channel, have changed in two-hundred-plus years.

According to *History of Coös County, New Hampshire*, by Georgia Drew Merrill (W.A. Fergusson, 1888), the original people of Coos County were the Iroquois, the Algonquins, and the Abenaki. Merrill says that the name Coos is derived from the Abenaki word *Cohos*, or *Coo-ash*, for "pines." The tribe occupying this region was known as the Coo-ash-aukes, or "dwellers in the pine tree country." During the early days of colonization by Europeans, the Native American people in this region were decimated by disease brought by the white settlers. When this was still their land, though, I am sure the Abenaki loved this area as much as we do today.

Today, the Grant is an eddy in time, where the flow of development has reversed itself, at least for the time being. It is a temporal backwater, swirling slowly in circles. For The Boys, this backwater is a refuge from the main current of our lives. And it is a refuge with a rich history. An eddy also is a great place to fish.

———

It is no surprise that there is plenty of flat water and fine paddling on the Dead Diamond River.

History is an important part of the Dartmouth experience. Beginning with freshman orientation, we heard the stories and songs about Eleazar Wheelock, who, in 1769, the year before the Boston Massacre, founded Dartmouth College to educate the "Indians." We were told about famous alumni like Daniel Webster, Robert Frost, Theodore Geisel ("Dr. Seuss"), and Nelson Rockefeller. (Future generations of "first-years" would learn of such notable alumnae as author Louise Erdrich, Senator Kirsten Gillibrand, and television producer Shonda Rhimes, but the College's first class including female students had yet to graduate when The Boys arrived in the fall of 1975.) We also learned of the Wheelock Succession, that line of Dartmouth presidents who have guided the College for centuries right up through the tumultuous transition to co-education, still the source of growing pains while we were undergrads. Since we're a naturally curious bunch, it should be no surprise that The Boys would be intrigued by the history of the Dartmouth Grant.

The Second College Grant is a curious name. "Okay, who granted what to whom?" and "Was there a first one?" you might wonder. Good questions. Wonder no more.

In 1789, the New Hampshire legislature provided Dartmouth

College the first grant, a piece of land in the current town of Clarksville, a ways north of the College in the upper Connecticut River Valley. This was a mechanism (though unsustainable) for funding higher education in the day. College founders sold off the land to support construction of the earliest buildings on the current site of Dartmouth Row, the College's signature line of white Georgian classroom buildings that flank the Dartmouth Green. By 1792, when the College needed additional funds, it petitioned the legislature for another grant of land. In 1807, after years of debate, the legislature agreed to Dartmouth's request but provided strict conditions for this second grant, which now appears on maps as an official township called Second College Grant.

According to the Act that granted the land, this "tract of land amounting to six miles square" could never be sold and "the incomes of such land shall be applied wholly and exclusively to assist the education of [New Hampshire] youths . . . to defray the expenses of an education at said seminary without such assistance." As a result, income from the Second College Grant is still used to support scholarships for New Hampshire students, and the land is still there for us to enjoy. While vehicle access is restricted, the land is open to the public for non-motorized use.

Originally, sections of the Grant were offered as 100-acre lots for long-term leasing, but few settlers were interested in farming this remote and rugged land, so not many lots were ever leased. In 1853, an agent hired by the College to evaluate the best uses of the Grant recommended a focus on timber harvesting. In hindsight, this doesn't seem so surprising, but perhaps the conclusion was revelatory at the time.

Soon after this decision, a sawmill was built at the mouth of the Diamond Gorge, and numerous log-driving dams were placed strategically on the Swift and Dead Diamond rivers and tributaries. The logging era was underway.

After the turn of the twentieth century, the College hired a forester to oversee timber harvesting at the Grant. As World War I ended, a major spruce budworm epidemic caused concern about the future value of the wood. As a result, the College issued a contract to the Brown Company of Berlin, New Hampshire, to cut all standing softwood. The extraordinary revenue earned from that large-scale cutting allowed the College to establish an endowment for scholarships for New Hampshire residents. Over the following decades the Grant has continued to produce timber and income. In 2014, woodcutting operations in the Grant generated a net revenue of about $300,000, and a similar amount was withdrawn from the timber endowment to fund scholarships.

Even though timber was clearly king, in the 1920s engineers proposed Diamond Gorge as a site for a hydropower dam that would have flooded tens of thousands of acres of timberland upstream from the Confluence. The plans called for a dike to be built in the saddle on the ridge to the west of Diamond Peaks in order to raise the overall water level above the current ridge line and create an enormous impoundment. Fortunately, nothing came of the project, but the Dike Site Road still leads up to the saddle west of Diamond Peaks, providing excellent cross-country skiing in winter.

The first vehicle access road into the Grant was built in 1944, allowing hardwood, mostly yellow birch and maple, to be harvested and sold in larger quantities. Hardwood doesn't float well, so it was unsuitable for log drives and had to be trucked from the Grant. Gate Camp was located at the entrance of the access road and overlooking the river, about a half mile north of Wentworth's Location. It is still used today and houses the only operating landline in the Grant. A fabulous patch of pink and white foxgloves blooms each summer on the hillside behind the cabin.

Shortly after the main road was built, Alder Brook Cabin was constructed several miles up the Swift Diamond River, marking the beginning of the Grant being used regularly by Dartmouth Outing Club (DOC) students for recreation. My brother and I stayed at Alder Brook for several days in March 1979 and found it quite cozy as we watched winter slowly turn to spring.

At what is now the intersection of the Swift Diamond and Dead Diamond roads, the Management Center was built in 1951 to provide sleeping quarters and an office for the College forester. Sam's Cabin, named for the Grant's first caretaker, Sam Brungot, was built across the road from the Management Center. These two cabins and their woodsheds form a cozy little "village" near the Confluence. The Management Center was eventually converted from a working office to the most spacious cabin in the Grant, with a big kitchen, three bunk rooms, and a large living/dining room.

Management Center Cook Stove. Watercolor & Ink by Phil Odence, 2004.

After several years staying in the Hellgate area, The Boys concluded that bunking in the Management Center simplified lugging our gear and beer to the cabin, and gave us easier access to more fishing options upstream in both rivers. Due to its history, the walls inside the Management Center display pictures commemorating several important events in the Grant, most notably a visit by President Dwight D. Eisenhower in June 1955. This is a story worth telling.

———

I first became aware of President Eisenhower's visit to the area when I was fishing the upper Magalloway River in the late 1980s with my buddy Lou Zambello. On a rock near Little Boy Falls, about thirty miles north of the Grant, a brass plaque commemorates Ike's fishing trip to the region. The pool below the falls is now called Eisenhower Pool. I was told by a local camp owner that Ike had fished there for several days while staying on Parmachenee Lake in Maine, the guest of Brown Paper Company CEO Lawrence Whittemore.

Hearing later that Ike had also visited the Grant, I assumed he had fished there as well. One day, while looking up at a photo in the Management Center and sipping my morning coffee, I started to think about Eisenhower's trip. Why had he come all the way to this remote corner of New England? Was he, the former president of Columbia University, buddies with Dartmouth President John Sloan Dickey? What brought him this far north, and how did he manage time away from the Cold War to go fishing? And, most importantly, did he catch any trout?

I did some research and discovered a vivid *Sports Illustrated* story from August 1955 about Eisenhower's Grant visit. That led me to peruse photos from the College archives, read yellowed clips of Maine newspaper articles, and download copies of the President's speeches delivered at the ski jump in Berlin, New Hampshire, and at a ceremony in Rangeley, Maine. Maria Fernandez, an intern in the Rauner Special Collections Library at Dartmouth, was very helpful in locating papers from President Dickey's archives that relate to the visit, including his correspondence with President Eisenhower. I even tracked down and spoke with two Dartmouth alumni, Stewart Sanders and Lincoln Yu, who were at the Grant as undergraduates on the day of the President's visit.

A clearer picture emerged. The story begins with Dartmouth awarding Ike an honorary degree at Commencement in 1953, a few months after he took office. His chief of staff, Sherman Adams, former governor of New Hampshire and member of the Dartmouth Class of 1920, had been a key player in Ike's surprise wins in the New Hampshire primary, at the Republican Convention, and ultimately (and more predictably) in the general election. The trustees decided to award an honorary degree to Governor Adams and then, at the suggestion of an undergraduate, Richard Cahn '53, went for the Daily Double by inviting President Eisenhower to Hanover at the same time to receive a similar honor. The President agreed on the condition that he would not be treated as the featured guest, although that was hardly a condition that could be met. During his time in Hanover, Ike stayed at President Dickey's home, and the two men (who were *not* close acquaintances previously) learned they shared passions for both international affairs and fly-fishing.

A few years later, while contemplating a run for re-election, the President and his team planned a swing through northern New England, and Governor Adams asked Sid Hayward, secretary of the College, to assist with the trip logistics. Realizing the route would pass nearby, Hayward, a Grant regular, found a way to get Ike to the Grant so he could take advantage of President Dickey's long-standing invitation to go fishing. Of course, POTUS came with a motorcade of Secret Service agents and politicians, not to mention the press corps. It must have been quite a spectacle.

As it turned out, due to his tight schedule, President Eisenhower had no time to actually fish with President Dickey. According to then-students Stewart Sanders and Lincoln Yu, Ike did not so much as wet a line. But, Eisenhower and entourage enjoyed a lunch that featured trout caught for them that morning, along with beans, cornbread, and pie. Ike helped cook the fish and swapped fishing stories with the sportsmen and students in attendance (virtually all men). He was also presented with a collection of flies tied by Sam Brungot, caretaker of the Grant.

What was going on in the world while Ike was kicking back at the Grant? Oh, this and that. The President had recently talked his Joint Chiefs of the Armed Forces out of a tactical nuclear strike on Communist China, over a stare-down with Formosa. From the trout streams, Ike would fly straight to Geneva for talks on nuclear disarmament with Russia and the European allies. The former Supreme Commander of the Allied Forces in Europe was also working hard to reduce military spending and balance the federal budget.

But first, Ike fished. Though not at the Grant. His fishing exploits at Little Boy Falls later that weekend made headlines around the world. Still, for a ninety-minute, low-key lunch that Saturday in the midst of the Cold War, the Dartmouth Grant was the center of the free world, even sporting a telephone hotline and newly strung wire connecting the Grant to Washington, DC, in the event of a nuclear attack or some other crisis.

————

A couple of other milestones for the Grant occurred during Eisenhower's second term. For one, The Boys were born. Not in the Grant, of course, but without the seven of us, this story would not be told.

Then, on the site of an old logging camp, Peaks Cabin was constructed to overlook the confluence of the Swift and the Dead Diamond rivers. During the spring following John Kennedy's swearing in to the White House, a Dartmouth Outing Club crew went to work on Merrill Brook Cabin, near the site of the old Upper Farm. Although distant from much of the better fishing, it's conveniently located near Monahan's Bathtub, which offers a cool dip to rinse off the bug dope and grime from hiking or mountain biking.

What visitors commonly call the Grant actually extends a bit north of the originally granted land. In fact, Hellgate Gorge is outside the Grant proper. In 1971, the College negotiated a recreation lease with the Brown Company for 10,600 acres of the Atkinson and Gilmanton Academy Grant to secure access to the scenic area around Hellgate.

Hellgate Gorge is a narrow slot through the bedrock ledge. It sits just above a series of small waterfalls that cascade into a large pool with some of the best rock-skipping stones on the planet. The College continued to lease the area despite multiple changes in its ownership and, in 1984, was able to purchase about 200 acres to lock in ownership of the Hellgate environs.

The Hellgate Hilton came about in 1972 to replace the decrepit logging camps located near where Amasa Ward had his fishing camp in the 1800s. The Hilton sits up on a hillside overlooking the field where Pete Blodgett Cabin is located now, just downstream of the big pool below the falls. Hellgate Gorge Cabin was built two years later on the road side of the river and has a spectacular view of the gorge.

Stoddard Cabin (for students) and Johnson Brook Cabin (for alumni) were built in 1987 and 1996, respectively, to handle the increased interest in the Grant by undergrads and alums. Stoddard is across the footbridge from Monahan's Bathtub, near a crossroads of rutted woods roads labeled on some maps as Diamond Four Corners.

Johnson Brook is located near Ellingwood Falls on the upper Swift Diamond, a few miles past Alder Brook Cabin.

————

One of the first things we do each trip is thumb through the cabin logbook to see who has visited during the past year. The logbooks, which were introduced in the 1950s, started as an official record of visitors entering the Grant on business or for special affairs. Log entries soon evolved to include first-person details about visitors' activities: wildlife sightings, musings, berry-picking, canoe trips, recipes, and even the occasional diagram for a jury-rigged mouse trap. They are authored by people of all ages and range from the distinctive hand of President John Sloan Dickey and the blocky print lettering of a child to longer entries in old-school cursive. Readers of these logs have to be impressed by how important this place is to so many people.

Three of the oldest logbooks in the collection are wood-bound volumes from the Management Center cabin, chronicling the years from the dedication of that building in September 1951 through the early 1970s. The first two signatures in the original log are those of Randolph Pack, president of the Pack Forestry Foundation which provided funds to build the facility, and Sid Hayward, secretary of the College. Dartmouth President Ernest Martin Hopkins is the eighth signature on the page. Perley Churchill, Class of 1907, for whom the first bridge over the Diamond River is named, was also in attendance.

These early logbooks also demonstrate the expanding scope of users of the new Management Center facility, including sixteen students and two professors on the first Geography Department field trip in October 1951; the dozens of members of Ike's entourage in June 1955; and eighty-nine Peace Corps trainees, African nationals, and French instructors in August 1965.

Many logbook entries are simple recitations of activities and fish caught. For instance, President Dickey and his family visited August 5-9, 1966, leaving the following logbook entry: "Family party—fished the Dead from farm down, [Management] Center up and above Slewgundy without any result except one caught by J. D., Jr. and a big one lost by him at the net. Water very low at about 65° . . . saw doe, two fawns, bear cub, beaver, grouse, etc. Great weather, some berries.

— John Dickey, Chris, Sukie, John Jr., Joan Dickey"

Others are philosophical and in tune with the times.

July 13, 1970:
"Groovin' vs. Exploring
Salvation vs. Consciousness
Maintain vs. Progress…
On the Road Again"
Michael A Stratton '69

In true Dartmouth spirit, many logbook entries are more personal, wry, and anecdotal. Entries from the 1980s and 90s include an impressive winter adventure by a spirited group of Grant veterans, the voice of a budding young nature lover, a bored family on a rainy day, and an understated couple marking the start of their new life together.

February 6-8, 1981: "Tenth Annual Interstate Geriatric Ski Tour and Grand Sub-Arctic Bushwhack — We did it! After all those years of false starts and vain attempts, all the increasingly difficult tours while our physical power gradually faded, we finally achieved the circumambulation of the Grant. . . Left camp at 6:30, headed for Hellgate. . . Twelve hours and ten minutes, just over twenty-four miles . . . a perfect day! Haute cuisine, as usual . . . —Peter Blodgett '74, John Richardson, Ed Chamberlain, Murray Washburn, Willem Lange."

September 3, 1983: "When we were getting out of the water there was a leech on my toe, I don't know how I discovered it! My sister Tracy came out with a giant laugh . . . While I was trying to flick the leech off of my toe I was yelling at my sister for laughing while I thought how gross this was. I finally got it off . . . Best wishes in your trip, Paula Young (11)."

August 22, 1997: "One rainy day we built mouse traps for mice and were surprised when we caught six mice. The traps that I was sure wouldn't work caught four mice, two at a time! —Laura (age 10), Nathan (age 8), Jan & Don Ebering"

January 17, 1999: "Got married just up the road and took photos by the cabin. —JR & KB"

And, finally, others evoke the mood of the trip, including the precious solitude. On July 18, 2005, Dan Nelson '75, shared his bliss by noting simply: "I think I have the Grant to myself tonight."

When full, the logbooks are placed into the College Archives for posterity. Phil and I visited the Rauner Library during our reunion in 2015, and spent an enjoyable hour or so digging through the old logbooks, searching for our own entries over the years and for others that shed light on the Grant and its visitors. The library houses the College's rare books collection, and I suppose the one-of-a-kind logbooks are among the rarest. We had to lock up our back-packs and surrender our driver's licenses before being presented with a couple of boxes of documents. It was a funny scene, spreading out those dog-eared, hand-written notebooks next to a copy of the Guten-berg Bible. Sadly, we have yet to find the entry from our first visit to Merrill Brook.

———

One thing I love about fly-fishing is that it is totally in the moment. It is almost impossible to think about work, or worries, or the future when you are casting, stripping line, and waiting for a strike. A zen break for Guy.

And I need it, because I do think about the future. All the time. In fact, I have spent my entire career working to solve environmental problems that transcend generations, to try to create a more sustain-able economy, and build a fair and tolerant society for our kids and grandkids.

Even though the Grant today is an eddy in time, I wonder what this place will be like in 50 or 100 years. How will climate change affect the ecosystem, the rivers, and the trout that depend on cold water to thrive? How will technology affect the Grant experience? Will it remain "off the grid" much longer, or in the long run will there even be a grid? Will these cabins and rivers always be a place of refuge and renewal?

This will be an interesting topic of conversation over dinner some night in the Management Center. I am hopeful that the College will maintain its stewardship of the land. That North Woods species like lynx, bald eagles, fishers, otters, native brook trout, northern jays, and tall white pines will continue to thrive here. That a child will delight in seeing a moose and catching a mouse, and be grossed out when her sister discovers a leech on her toe.

Finally, I hope that another group of Dartmouth alumni, perhaps including some grandchildren of The Boys, will be writing in the logbooks about their fly-fishing adventures after twenty years running.

Of Wild Rivers and Wild Trout

By David Van Wie

Not only are the trout wild up here, so are the rivers.
After twenty-some years, we know we can fish in the same
place on the same weekend of the year and never get the same
conditions twice in ten years. Some years we get low water, cold and
clear as crystal. Other years, the flow may be fast and cloudy but still
wadeable. The rock where I caught my biggest trout last year might be
underwater this year. The deep pool we fished one June is a shallow
run the next year. Or, after an overnight rainstorm, the rock I stood on
yesterday is lost beneath a swirl and a wave today.

Now and then, we get a total blowout: the river rises so high we
aren't sure if the roads will be flooded or washed out, and we wonder
whether we can make it home. A few of The Boys will readily admit we
wouldn't mind getting "stuck" in the Grant an extra few days.

Human disturbance in the Swift Diamond and Dead Diamond
watersheds is limited to logging, dirt roads, and a handful of rustic
cabins. These rivers are fairly unusual, even in northern New England,
because there are no dams and no towns between the source and
the outlet below the gorge. The shorelines and wetlands are virtually
untouched. While the Grant's logging history has had an impact on the
river (sediment and temperature in particular, according to Grant histo-
rian Jack Noon), the water quality is pristine and the flow unfettered,
fully subject to the whims of the weather. The weather patterns—rainy
days, thunderstorms, heat waves, or dry spells—determine the flow and
temperature of the water, which, combined, have a big impact on the
fishing.

The weather in the northern mountains of New Hampshire is
inscrutable. We have had sweltering days in June, shivering wet days in
July, and cold fronts that blow in from Canada at any time dropping

the temperature twenty degrees in an hour. We anticipate the potential pendulum swing when packing for the Grant. Our gear includes bathing suits and flip flops, as well as fleece and winter jackets. Some people can be fooled by the weather at home while they are prepping for the trip. But the hills of Coos County are a world away, and the weather will sometimes catch us off guard.

The unpredictable conditions are a big part of what makes the fishing such a challenge in the Grant—and very rewarding when we have success. Like backgammon or cribbage, fishing is a pleasing mixture of skill and luck. A great run can be spoiled by a bad draw on the weather. We have to be ready to take the good with the bad, and appreciate good fortune when it comes our way.

———

The terrain in the watersheds of the Swift Diamond and Dead Diamond rivers is rocky and hilly. Mountainous would be an exaggeration, as the hills in the Grant are all less than 3,000 feet. But the effect of the terrain is that the rivers (as we've learned firsthand) are very "flashy"—when it rains, the rivers rise quickly. When it stops raining, the rivers drop, but not as quickly as they rise.

Being an environmental scientist, I am a glutton for interesting data. Happily for me, there is a US Geological Survey river gage station in the Diamond River at the mouth of the gorge, and (oh, this is so cool) the flow data are published online in real time! The gage automatically measures the river's depth and speed, and, based on the surveyed shape of the channel through the rock, calculates the amount of water traveling through the gorge. So a data geek like me can check in, even from my desk at work, to see how the river is flowing at any given moment.

In the week or two before our trip, I watch the weather maps and the river flow to try to predict what conditions we can expect. Despite the one certainty that things can change overnight, it's fun to anticipate what might happen. Mr. Compulsive Data Geek (that would be me) even snaps screen shots of the flow graphs and sends them to The Boys. I'm pretty sure they don't get as excited about this information as I do, but they indulge me nevertheless. (For examples of the flow data graphs, see the "Extra Credit" material at the end of this chapter.)

The river flow from the mouth of Diamond Gorge is not always this calm and fishable.

Yes, I get the irony in having online instant data capability for the Diamond River, because once we get near the Grant, we are off the grid. No electricity, no cell service, no Internet. So what happens the day or two after we arrive can still be a mystery. Surprises still surprise us, especially with early summer storms. That is part of the fun, going from the known to the unknowable, transitioning from modern technology to the mysteries of nature.

When the river rises quickly, the water gets cloudy with silt. The current can be treacherous, if not impossible to fish in most places. This can make us Boys very unhappy. One year when high water left us all skunked and frustrated, we gave up on the Grant and drove an hour or so over to Kennebago and Parmachenee lakes in Maine to fish the flatwater. We had some success catching trout and landlocked salmon, as well as some relief from our frustration, but it felt like cheating.

Each trip, we adjust our fishing strategy to the flow du jour. Can we float dry flies with a dead drift in a slow-moving pool? Are the trout even rising in this flow, or will the faster current mean we have to fish streamers with sinking line behind the rocks and in the eddies?

As the conditions change from year to year, our success in

catching trout can be just as unpredictable. Some years, we think the water conditions are ideal, but we have little success. Other years, we fret about the water conditions, but manage to catch a fair number of lovelies. And the size of the fish we catch can be all over the map.

In 2011, Dartmouth began working with the New Hampshire Fish and Game Department, Trout Unlimited, and other local sportsmen's groups to conduct a major study of migration and spawning patterns of native brook trout. Brook trout, some of which weighed up to four pounds (four pounds!), were captured in the Swift Diamond and Dead Diamond rivers and implanted with radio telemetry tags to track their movements throughout the watershed. The study team is trying to determine the extent to which brook trout in the Swift and Dead Diamond represent different populations from brook trout elsewhere in the Magalloway watershed.

As a result of the fieldwork, the team has learned that individual fish may travel more than fifty miles, leaving the Grant and migrating into the Magalloway and Rapid rivers in Maine, then returning to the Grant, and sometimes even dropping back down into Umbagog Lake for the winter. This new study is helping the New Hampshire Fish and Game, the Maine Department of Inland Fisheries and Wildlife, and Dartmouth make future management decisions to ensure the preservation and enhancement of these last remaining populations of wild brook trout in the region.

Even though there are some big fish in the river, they are rare. I tell first-time fishermen to the Grant to set their Thrill-O-Meter at eight inches, and if they catch anything bigger than that, it is okay to brag and celebrate. After more than twenty years, we still haven't figured this place out. I think I speak for all of The Boys in saying that we actually enjoy the mystery, even if it means lousy fishing now and then.

———

With all the changing conditions at the Grant, the one constant is the fish. They are beautiful. Beautiful and enigmatic. Wary and lightning quick in their underwater world, the trout are formidable quarry.

Moreover, the brook trout at the Dartmouth Grant are all wild native fish. Fully wild trout are rare now in the eastern US, where hatchery-raised trout have been stocked and often breed with native trout in most water bodies. But this has not happened in the Grant for many decades. Natural selection is in full force here, and the fishermen reap the rewards. Wild trout can be very wary and spooky. Or very hungry and naïve, depending on the conditions.

The trout's colors are incredible, especially their spots. Each spot—whether it's red, yellow, green, blue, or gold—has a lighter-shaded ring around the center color. Set against a background of bronze and green, the spots call to mind the way pointillist painters use small but distinct patches of color that the viewer's eye interprets as a unified image. The spots and splotches provide excellent camouflage in a rocky stream with sand, shadows, and a gravel bottom.

The totality of color transitions from dark bronze, on the trout's back, to lighter bronze or taupe, on the sides, to yellow on the belly. Unlike a leopard, a brook trout can actually change its spots (or at least the shades and contrasts) during the season, as it moves from place to place, and from year to year, as it grows from a fingerling to a parr to a mature fish. In the fall, the underside colors of spawning fish turn a deep orange, almost red. A mature brook trout in spawning colors is a magnificent sight to behold.

————

The human's terrestrial world above meets the trout's liquid world below on a flowing plane. For a fly fisherman like me, the only connection between human existence and the trout's submerged realm is a 6X tippet, a nearly invisible fluorocarbon line only .005 inches thick. To be sure, it's a tenuous connection between our worlds. When I catch a trout, bringing it from the underwater world into my domain above the surface, I marvel at it for the few seconds it is in my net or in my hand. I then release it to swim away and disappear.

"You can't outsmart a cold-blooded fish?" asks my wife. "Well, yes I can, fairly often," I reply. "But not always," I add, though only to myself.

"But they have a brain smaller than a pea," she correctly points out.

"And that is precisely what makes it so hard for me to think like a trout." This really cracks her up.

The first rule of fishing is "fish to fish." By this I mean: cast your line where you know (or strongly suspect) a fish might be. There is no point in casting to where there are no fish. This may seem obvious, but many fishermen don't seem to get it. If I want to actually catch a fish, there must be at least one fish in the vicinity of where I am casting. Simple enough.

But, instead of determining where the fish are holding and what might interest them, some fisherman choose a pool with little thought and blindly cast in the hopes of happening upon a fish. Or they believe that a fish might just wander by, perhaps on a Sunday stroll. When I was young and didn't know better, that is exactly what I did. Needless to say, I didn't have much luck using this low percentage strategy.

Knowing where fish are hiding, and, even better, actively feeding, is more than half the battle. If I don't know for certain where they are, then I should have a pretty darned good idea based on past experience. Even if the trout are right there where I think they are, they might not be interested in taking a fly. But knowing a trout is there is better than the alternative, which is pure guesswork. Or dumb luck.

Resting on the bottom of the stream among the shadows, trout remain almost invisible even to a seasoned fly fisherman. They are very good at hiding because there are many hungry predators with a sharp eye and lethal tactics—otters, kingfishers, mergansers, mink, herons, osprey, and eagles, as well as other bigger fish. When a trout rises to investigate a fly, it sometimes turns a bit, "flashing" its lighter belly. That flash can be enough to give away its hiding place. Once I know a fish is interested in my fly, I just have to figure out what exactly I need to do to get that trout (or its neighbor) to take my fly with conviction.

Light and shadows, temperature, flow, cover (rocks, logs, cut banks, or other structure), and food availability are the main factors that determine where a trout will be. Ultimate survivalists, trout need oxygen, food, and cover, in that order. Their existence is all about optimizing those factors while expending less energy getting the food than the amount of energy the food provides.

Trout prefer cooler water, between 40° and 60°F. Cold water contains more oxygen than warm water. Trout seek water with higher oxygen levels either by moving to areas with cooler water temperature or where the water is physically aerated, such as beneath a small waterfall. If the river water warms up on a hot day, as it does quickly on the

Swift Diamond, the trout will hunker down where groundwater (averaging 42° to 52°F in northern New Hampshire) seeps in through the gravel, usually in the deeper holes.

For food, there are several options: insects (either aquatic or terrestrial of various types and life stages), other smaller fish, worms, leeches, fish eggs, and a few other small animals, including frogs. A big trout might eat the tiniest insects and swallow something as large as a mouse. I caught the biggest trout I ever caught (three-plus pounds) on the smallest fly I have ever used, which was about the size of a flea. When I netted it, the trout looked like it had a poppy seed stuck in its teeth. Smaller fish must eat smaller food, but can occasionally be quite ambitious in what size bug or fish they will go after. It's a wonder how a little fish can get its mouth around a formidable #8 size streamer fly.

In a river, the moving current provides a traveling cafeteria line of food options that concentrate in certain places, depending on the flow patterns and eddies around rocks. The menu will include whatever small creatures are hatching, migrating, or drifting by. The trout's main job, then, is to find a cool place with good cover from predators, with not too much current (to save energy) that's near a steady flow that might bring food right past its nose.

To take advantage of this moving cafeteria effect, I try to place my fly in the seam that is often visible between fast water and slow water, near rocks, or above pockets deep enough for a trout to hide in. Often we "fish the foam line," where natural foam, debris, and floating bugs concentrate into a predictable path down the stream. The trout will compete with each other for the most advantageous resting places near these fast-food locations, and dart out to take a morsel as it floats by.

As stuff passes by in the current, the trout has to decide in an instant: is it Food or Not Food? A creature of habit and often short on memory, the fish will often choose the familiar, but may investigate new items that could be Food. I sometimes change flies five or ten times trying to find one that a trout will think is a real meal. It can be harder to trick them in clear water than in cloudy water because the trout may get a better look at the fly and easily decide it is Not Food.

Trout will often lock on to one type of bug that is most abundant, especially when thousands of that insect are hatching at once. Large concurrent hatches are a survival strategy for various insect species. If

I can mimic the trout's favorite food du jour with a specific fly, then a strike by the trout is more likely. This is called "matching the hatch." Hitting a big hatch, as Phil and Bill Burgess did their first evening in the Grant, is a fisherman's dream because trout will congregate into a feeding frenzy. Meanwhile I am rummaging through my vest to quickly find the right fly that looks like the natural insect on the water.

Not only is the choice of artificial fly important, so is the "presentation." A wild trout can quickly tell the difference between a real insect drifting naturally in the current compared to an artificial fly that is dragging cross-wise to the flow because it is connected to a heavier line and rod. How a dry fly rests on the surface, or how a streamer "swims" through the current, or how deep it sinks in the water column—these are all important aspects of the skill it takes to entice a trout to take an artificial fly made of feathers, hair, and a hook.

To be successful, The Boys need to know a good bit about bugs (entomology), trout (ichthyology), river ecology, hydrology, and physics. And beer. Either as a break from the concentration needed to fly fish for hours at a time, as a reward to celebrate the day's catch, or as solace for getting skunked on the outing, somehow a beer is an essential part of the equation.

Above all, The Boys and I have learned that the most important thing about chasing wild trout in wild rivers is to enjoy every minute of it.

––––––––

Extra Credit: What the River Gage Shows

Hey, there. Mr. Compulsive Data Geek Environmental Scientist here again, with some actual data from the river. I won't take it personally if you skip this part to get to the next story. Really, I won't. But you might find this interesting.

The US Geological Survey's gage measures the combined flow of the rivers below Diamond River Gorge in cubic feet per second, or cfs. (A cubic foot of water is about 7.5 gallons.) This is the total amount of water flowing past the gage on an instantaneous basis. The gage also measures the river depth in feet at that point of the river.

The flow patterns over a month might seem fairly predictable, but they really aren't. Every spring is different, and things change in a hurry. Every now and then a storm will stall over the valley and dump a few inches in an hour or two. An inch of rain, when funneled down through the valley, might cause the river to rise a foot or more.

A graph of the river flow from June 2014 looks like this:

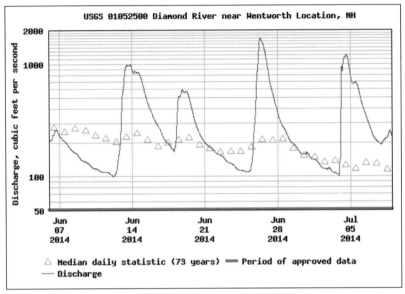

The Diamond River flow graph shows a rollicking ride in June 2014. From USGS website.

The typical flow for June is between 100 and 250 cfs. The graph shows that the river rises sharply with a storm, sometimes from 100 cfs to 1,000 cfs or 2,000 cfs in a matter of hours. The river then drops at a fairly steady rate of about 65 to 75 percent in the first 24 hours, and then by another half again in the second 24 hours.

Note that each horizontal line on the graph is 100 cfs and that the flow graph is *logarithmic,* so the lines get closer and closer together at higher values. If this were regular graph paper, the spikes would be much higher relative to the typical or median flow.

In depth (feet) at the gage, the graph looks like this:

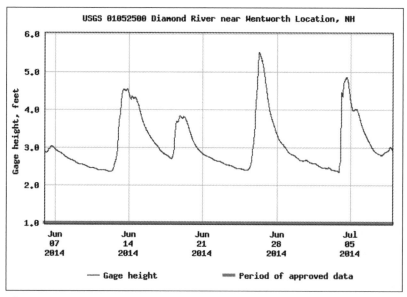

The Diamond River depth goes from wadeable to treacherous and back again in June 2014. From USGS website.

On the second graph, we can see that the river rose from 2.5 feet (about waist deep) to 5.5 feet (up to our eyeballs) deep virtually overnight on June 25 and 26. Because of the shape of the river channel, a rise from 3 to 4 feet might mean double the flow in cfs. A rise from 4 to 5 feet might actually be 4 or 5 times the flow. That means about twice as much water is traveling more than twice as fast. The water drains out of the valley very quickly, sort of like a big flush. And the cycle starts again when the next storm comes along.

The Hellgate Years

By Phil Odence

In several of the early years we stayed in the Hellgate Gorge area, mostly at the cabin known as the Hellgate Hilton. The beautiful hillside view and great pool for swimming right out front make for very pleasant accommodations. Hellgate Gorge is about ten miles north of the Management Center, which, on the bumpy, winding Dead Diamond Road translates to about thirty additional minutes entering and departing the Grant.

Despite the Hilton's charms, we've opted in recent years for function over form. Staying at the Management Center or Sam's Cabin makes for a shorter trip and easier access to fishing. Moving south also had the benefit of allowing us to explore farther upstream on the Swift with less travel time. It is only in the last decade that we have visited three of the most beautiful sites in the Grant. The 2,400-foot Diamond Peaks, reached via a trailhead across from Sam's Cabin, offers a vast panorama on a clear day. Sam's Lookout, atop a 100-foot cliff a few miles west, affords a stunning view to the west, upstream along the Swift. It's especially vivid at sunset. And, Ellingwood Falls, a few miles farther upstream, is a scenic maze of water raging over a series of granite ledges.

But we were pretty attached to the Hilton, despite its challenging location—the cabin was located on the other side of the river and more than 100 yards from the road. A decade ago, the Outdoor Programs office constructed a marvelous suspension walking bridge. That, combined with a couple of lawn carts, has eased the burden of hauling gear across the Dead Diamond. Before the bridge, we managed, though it wasn't easy.

A short hike from Hellgate Gorge to Finnson's Cliff offers a fine view of Hellgate Hilton.

Often the river was low enough to ford, and for those first few years, we waded. Nowadays I still bring all my gear to the Grant in a 1970s-era frame pack, a habit left over from our early years hiking through water and gravel bars from the car to the cabin. A vivid memory: my ol' San Francisco roommate, Saul Levy '73, showed up for a night at the Grant after his twenty-fifth reunion. It was a sunny and warm afternoon when The Boys spotted "the Mayor of Saulsville" coming down the bank. As he waded in the knee-deep water, he stopped halfway through his ford and smiled. Then, standing straight like a soldier, he toppled himself, fully clothed and still smiling, into the drink.

But the "official" way to cross, before the suspension bridge, was to employ an old flat-bottomed duck boat that was tied to a tree up the bank, on the road side of the river. After rowing to the opposite shore, you would haul the metal craft up onto a bank of cobblestone-size rocks, cross the rocks, and then truck your gear up the steep, grassy ascent to the cabin.

After a couple of years of human drayage, we noted some tire tracks on the bank and thereby discovered that it was possible to navigate an

SUV down the steep path, across the river, and onto the cobble beach—much closer to the cabin. Not only a huge convenience, but also a rare opportunity to exercise the manly four-wheel-drive feature of an SUV.

Bill Burgess' Cherokee was the only vehicle we ever tried it with, and it managed like a champ. We took her back and forth a number of times. When traversing the river on the way back to the road, the Cherokee would pick up a quantity of water in the undercarriage, which drained as it ascended the dirt path. Thus, the path became wetter and slicker through the weekend, finally causing a minor mishap when, try as it might, the little engine couldn't quite make it up the steep bank without spinning its wheels. We had to jump out and push and pull, back and forth, and yank until, at the peak of our desperation, a passing Chevy Suburban, outfitted with a tow chain, hauled us up to the road. Phew!

———

We left the Cherokee on the road side that night—and a very good thing we did. That night we got an impressive lesson in North Country hydrology. It had been raining on and off since our arrival, and in two days, the river had risen a few inches, which had contributed to the Jeep's deposition of water onto the bank. But the water level was still low enough that even without the vehicle, we continued to ford on foot.

The rain became steadier that night, although still nothing to speak of, or so we thought. And so it was that we were dumbstruck when the sun rose the next morn and revealed that our placid little swimming hole had tripled in size, inundating the rock field, and was now drained by a raging torrent at the ford, all of which lay between us and the far shore.

Had there been a radical shift in the weather, this dramatic transformation might have been more understandable, but it had been raining for days. What triggered all this? Why now? Was it time to build an ark?

It is at such times as this when it is particularly helpful to have our very own environmental scientist, Professor Guy, along. He likened the local watershed to a 50,000-acre sponge. It had allowed some of the previous days' rain to pass through while soaking up the bulk of it.

At around the time of our last beer the night before, the sponge had reached saturation, and from then on, every drop that fell in the Dead Diamond's valley was one more drop in the river. And those drops, including perhaps a downpour or two somewhere farther upstream, resulted in the dramatic scene we now witnessed.

After considering our options for crossing back to the other side, Bob took one for the team and stripped off his clothes, plunging naked into the pecker-shriveling water. He swam across the river to retrieve the boat, which was, we thanked our lucky stars, still securely tethered to the tree. For both swimming and rowing, safety required an elliptical route, bending around upstream of the lay line in order to avoid being sucked down the raging flume at the tail of the pool. Had we, as was oft our habit, just pulled the duck boat up onto the cabin side rocks, now covered shin deep in river, we'd not only have been literally up the creek without a paddle, but also without a boat. Surely the vessel would already have been well past the Management Center (ten miles downstream) and on its way towards Umbagog Lake.

And then there was the Cherokee itself. We easily could have left it parked on the rocky beach for the night. At best it would have been up to the gunnels and probably a week away from being able to exit the Grant. At worst, it might have been trailing the boat southward, though I imagine it would have hung up on some rocks or a tree well before reaching Umbagog.

Another Phew! Once we loaded the cars, the next challenge was to find our way out of the Grant by an alternate route because parts of the main road were also flooded. Each of us felt fortunate to make it home more or less on time for Fathers' Day celebrations.

The Quartermaster's Lament

By Bob Chamberlin

Veg-All has become the ultimate symbol of thankless tasks.

Veg-All
Serving Up Memories Since 1926

While its nutritional benefits are legendary, Veg-All mixed vegetables bring something just as important to the table . . . convenience. Each can of Veg-All has the perfect blend of carrots, potatoes, green beans, corn and lima beans. . . It's the easy solution to any recipe dilemma. Just open and enjoy!
—from the Veg-All website

The task of supplying the Grant trip with food fell to me soon after I joined the group. Initially it had been Phil's job, because he lived in Hanover and was the chief cook. But the year after my first trip, he left the Upper Valley of New Hampshire to move back to Boston and asked if I could help him out by shopping for food. Feeling the need to further ingratiate myself with the veterans, I accepted. It quickly became clear why Phil was so eager to jettison the task. It was thankless. No matter what you did, there were complaints. Too much of this, too little of that. Why did you buy this and not that? You forgot the butter? We're out of *what*? A little like the Utah Phillips song about moose turd pie, but in that ditty, a complaint about the food resulted in cooking duty the next night. Not so here.

Interestingly, the quartermaster responsibilities have never included breakfast. Guy always takes care of that. That tradition started because he raised chickens and always had a surplus of eggs. He kept at it because . . .well, we don't change much. Guy's breakfast sandwiches are a highlight of the weekend—fried egg, ham, pepper jack cheese, grilled asparagus, and (the signature ingredient) ranch dressing, all on an English muffin. Not a bad start for a day of fishing. French toast with blueberries is another favorite—with local maple syrup, of course (it absolutely must be real maple syrup or Billy becomes despondent).

My first year as quartermaster, Phil laid out my duties and, to help me get going, handed me a worn-out, handwritten shopping list to use as a starting point. What impressed me immediately about the list was the range, quality, and quantity of food and drink. Until then, my experience in backwoods dining had been the can-o'-beans variety.

Top of the list was beer: one six-pack per person per day. Easy. "Make sure to buy some cans that can be stowed in a fishing vest. Make it Bud," Phil emphasized. Budweiser connects us to college days and, without fail, provokes a "why do we buy this stuff?" from Norm. Year after year, I buy Budweiser and then wait for Norm's reaction, like checking something off my to-do list. These days I bring along several different craft brews as well to please the ever-expanding range of palates, but I bring Bud, too. There's always Bud.

We don't get too fancy with dessert. I buy cookies. Oreos work well. I offset them with a bag of apples and another bag of carrots that usually go uneaten, but it helps to maintain the illusion that nutrition matters.

Actually, the dinners are pretty healthy. When I assumed the role of quartermaster, I was particularly impressed that the shopping list included salad. Packaged mixed greens are good and convenient. We've added tasty and expensive condiments and artisanal treats over time, including high-end olives, capers, roasted sunflower seeds, and Vermont cheeses. You get the idea: the food has gotten better and healthier over the years.

———

The list goes on. Two big bags of tortilla chips and plenty of salsa. A jar of peanuts. And more salsa. Boxes of granola or energy bars to stuff into our fishing vests. They go well with Budweiser.

Part of the list is organized by meal. These foodstuffs seem to have become immutable standards, such as grilled chicken and rice pilaf for the first night's dinner and Norm's chicken quesadillas (with leftover chicken) for the first lunch. ("Don't forget the scallions, or Norm will blow a cork," Phil cautioned on his list.)

Night Two brings Phil's masterpiece dinner which he changes-up from year to year, sometimes with an old favorite, other times with something new. Big hits have been his Bucatini Ameritriciana (the American backwoods version of amatriciana), traditional spicy chili, and Santa Fe Green Chili, which he reverse-engineered after a trip to the Southwest.

The challenge for the quartermaster is the demands these meals put on the shopping. It's dizzying to keep up with the ever-evolving list of requirements, and inevitably there is some disconnect which, however minor, sets Phil off (but in a friendly way). In a big dish, how important can one little ingredient be? Or two?

One year, in the rush through the supermarket, I forgot to pick up red pepper flakes for the amatriciana. You would have thought I'd caused a nuclear disaster. In the spirit of constructive criticism, Phil pointed with the carving knife in his hand at "½ tsp. red pepper flakes" in the printed email I'd unwisely pulled out to support my case. A half teaspoon . . . c'mon man! With some artistic modification, Phil produced what I thought was a perfectly delicious pasta dish, maybe even better than normal amatriciana. At some point, Phil began anticipating my omissions by bringing his own essential spices in little Ziploc bags. It's probably for the best.

––––––––

This brings me to the topic of my personal contribution to the culinary evolution of The Boys' trip: Veg-All. Generally speaking, we have always been on our game with respect to meat and pasta and hearty breakfasts. Supplying vegetables is a bit of a challenge, though, as one of the constraints that burdens the quartermaster is limited refrigerated storage, much of which is devoted to keeping the one six-pack per person per day cool for each of my compadres. Also, the propane-powered refrigerators at the Grant have a tendency to freeze fresh vegetables (which is somehow construed as a failure of the quartermaster).

One year I purchased frozen vegetables to combat this issue. In the rush to store the food before heading out to the stream, the frozen vegetables got put somewhere other than the iced-up freezer box.

Come dinnertime, Klingon happened upon the orange green mush in the defrosted bag. His look of disgust is one I will never forget. The following year I determined to solve the vegetable problem another way.

Which is what led me to discover Veg-All. You may be able to find it somewhere on your supermarket shelf. Or not. But don't look for it at Trader Joe's or Whole Foods. You'll need to be at one of those generic 65,000-square-foot supermarkets—Shaw's, Price Chopper, Walmart, or the like. It's been around since 1926. Check the lower shelves. I wouldn't be surprised if they're still selling the original cans. (Hard to know—no freshness dates back then.)

Veg-All comes in a 29-ounce can whose label depicts a cornucopia of wonderfully shiny vegetables: green beans and carrots, potatoes, corn, and lima beans. When you open a can, however, you are greeted by a sight that makes the aforementioned defrosted vegetable glob look downright garden fresh. There in a muddy broth are saturated pre-cooked vegetable entities brined in enough salt to kill a snake on contact. In an emergency, Veg-All has its attributes. For example, it can be mashed for use as spackling compound or, more constructively, as "clean fill" in a construction project. Not great eating though.

I am not sure if any of The Boys actually ate the Veg-All I generously provisioned for them that year, but my attempt at culinary exploration will never be forgotten. In fact, Veg-All has become the ultimate symbol of all thankless tasks. I know that every year I will, without fail, be reminded of the Veg-All faux pas—always worth a laugh. To show what a good sport I am and to keep the gag alive, I usually bring along a "fresh" can. One of the most demanding tasks of the quartermaster is determining quantities, but one can never buy too little Veg-All.

With only ten short years until the centennial anniversary of Veg-All, we will have to begin planning our celebration soon.

———

Bucatini Ameritriciana
Serves 7

1 Tbsp. butter
1 Tbsp. olive oil
2 cloves garlic, finely chopped
½ small onion, finely chopped
½ tsp. red pepper flakes
¼ lb. pancetta, finely chopped
1 28-oz. can tomatoes, ground in a blender
1 6-oz. can tomato paste
Salt
Pepper
½ tsp. sage
½ cup parsley, finely chopped
1 lb. bucatini pasta
Romano cheese for grating
Fresh basil

Melt butter and olive oil together in small saucepan. Add garlic and onion and red pepper flakes and cook over medium heat for five minutes.

Add pancetta and cook until fairly crisp, about ten minutes. Turn up heat if necessary, but be careful not to burn.

Add tomatoes and tomato paste, ½ tsp. salt, ½ tsp. pepper, sage, and parsley.

Stir to blend, and turn down heat to simmer. Cook for a half hour.

Cook a pound of bucatini (pasta with the hole in the middle of it). Drain when cooked, and add 1 Tbsp. butter. Mix thoroughly.

Serve pasta with the ameritriciana sauce, a lot of romano cheese, and chopped basil. Add salt and pepper to taste.

Green Chili

Serves 7

2.5 lbs. ground pork
Olive oil
2 medium onions, chopped
8 cloves garlic, mashed
1 Tbsp. oregano
2 tsp. cumin
3 bay leaves
1 15-oz. canned chopped mild green chiles
3 fresh mild green chiles
5 large potatoes, diced
2 15.5 oz. cans chicken broth
Salt
1 jar hot salsa verde (Mrs. Renfro's is very good)

Brown pork in Dutch oven.
Chop onions, mash garlic cloves, dice potatoes, and chop chiles.
Remove pork, and sauté onions in a little olive oil.
Once onions are translucent, return meat to Dutch oven.
Add potatoes, garlic, oregano, cumin, bay leaves, canned and fresh chiles, and chicken broth.
Cook for several hours.
Add salt and hot salsa verde to taste.
Serve with warmed corn tortillas or cornbread.

Catch and Release

By Phil Odence and David Van Wie

Wild trout are delicious. In a rustic camp, pan-fried is the way to go. Butter and pepper in a cast-iron skillet and a little lemon if you have it. The meat is delicate, flaky, and mild, and it melts in your mouth. With a little practice, you can deftly peel off the fine, colorful skin and remove the pinkish-gray flesh by flicking the fork parallel to the tiny bones. You get boneless morsels and leave nothing but a dainty skeleton.

The Boys all love trout, but we almost never eat them in the Grant. Maybe once every few years. Seriously. Some may assume that our catch is for consumption, but that's not how we roll.

Rather, we are proponents of the catch-and-release ethic, doing our best to return the fish unharmed to the river, to watch them dart off and hide in the waters from whence they came. We like to think of our excursions as "visiting the fish" and that we are simply seeking to have a brief interlude with them before we go back to our business and they to theirs. Sort of like visiting a piscine Oracle or the Dalai Lama with fins.

On the few occasions we have kept a fish it is usually because we have inadvertently injured it and realize that the poor creature has suffered too much trauma to return it to the water. The best way to honor the fellow's memory, we've determined, is to sauté and share him as a special hors d'oeuvre.

Fortunately, injuries to fish are infrequent, and the odds of the fish being sizable enough to share are small, so when you multiply them together. . . Well, we don't keep many, and it's been a few years since we haven't put one back.

The Boys aren't left-wing radical fish huggers. It's a question of circumstance. Many of us are happy to eat plentiful saltwater fish. When Guy lived in Wyoming years ago, he would catch a chunky rainbow trout for dinner about once a week from the Shoshone River down behind his office. And Phil likes to tell the tale of a fatal trout encounter he and Billy had years before that, which we'll share in Phil's own words:

In September of 1977, Billy and I set out from Philadelphia in my Toyota Corolla Liftback aimed for points west. We would drive 23,000 miles in eleven weeks. Our drive would take us from the depths of gambling tables in Las Vegas and dive bars in Pojoaque, New Mexico, to the summits of Nob Hill and various 14,000-foot peaks. We would encounter drug addicts, Mexican hustlers, and imaginary Swiss women (long story), as well as nuclear scientists and future senators and Olympic silver medalists.

It's an epic tale, and the full scope of those adventures is sufficient fodder for another written work, not this one.

In early October, a few weeks into our journey, we found ourselves with packs on our backs, slogging through deep snow atop Montana's Sperry Glacier. Sperry extends into Gunsight Pass in the central northern part of Glacier National Park, just south of the Canadian border. On the western side of the pass was Snyder Lake beside which we would lay our heads that night. Perhaps we were a little out of shape from two weeks of driving. At any rate, we were exhausted and starving when it came time to make camp after that first day of hiking. It was to be a several-day trip, and we had stocked up on your normal crappy camping food. But, while not hunter-gatherers, we were guys ready to chomp on some real live protein.

For years I carried, in one of the outer pockets of my old frame pack, a rudimentary fishing kit. It comprised a black and gray plastic 35-mm film canister (a container that someone rifling through my pack might have thought contained something else), a wine cork wrapped in monofilament, a small paper packet containing a half-dozen hooks, and several split-shot lead sinkers.

Once our tent was pitched and our bags were pulled from their stuff sacks to fluff up, we decided, with no great hopes, to see if we could pull a fish from Snyder Lake. We fashioned a crude drop line rig on a fat stick using the cork bobber, a couple of sinkers, and a hook. Having no luck finding a patch of soil rich enough to support worms, we were able to scrounge a hunk of medium sharp cheddar from our meager larder. From the shore, the weight of the sinkers allowed us to swing the end of the line back and forth enough to get a good toss, maybe fifteen or twenty feet out into the lake.

It seemed a long shot, but soon—it might even have been the first "cast"— we had a bite that turned into a beautiful ten-inch trout. In all we caught six or eight equally good-sized fish. And then we stopped, because we had enough. Billy cleaned the catch while I fired up the same one-burner compact Coleman stove I use to this day. We pan-fried the fish in some canola oil from a small squeeze bottle. The fry pan was half of a Boy Scout mess kit that I'd bought at an Army-Navy store (and which also continues to accompany me to the backwoods). I also travel with small vials of salt and pepper, enough to season a terrific meal. It's called catch and chow down.

That hike and that meal are among my fondest backwoods memories. I am less fond of the memory of the eight-inch snowfall that night, our collapsed tent, and our frigid retreat. That, too, is a story for another tome.

————

Catch and release is not a new concept, although relatively so given fishing's ancient history. The caveman who first figured out how to get a fish out of a stream had only one thing in mind. In those days before taxidermists and digital cameras, the best recognition he might receive was a grunt from his wife at the size of his catch and the size of the meal. But today, in the developed world anyway, few people fish our lakes and streams to feed the family, even here in New England, although it does happen. Billy and Phil's circumstance was a clear exception. For most fishermen, it's really about the sport. Catch-and-release fishing is the logical extension.

The concept was pioneered in England in the nineteenth century. That little country was on the cutting edge of sport fishing and the modern-day problem of bumping into constraints in natural resources (which is why they went off and started an empire). With the human population outstripping the kingdom's fish population, early conservationists realized that limiting the take was the only way to preserve fish stocks.

This healthy young brookie was fooled by Guy's Hornberg and is now ready to release. Photo by Dorothy Diggs.

In those days, our land was still a great wilderness and virtually all resources were in great abundance. You could dump whatever you needed to dump from the sparsely populated shores of a river, and the water would purify itself before it reached the next dumper. Plus, there was no shortage of fish. Around about the early part of the twentieth century, however, the burgeoning population led to more people with leisure time and, so, more fishermen. Combined with the shrinking miles of healthy fish habitats, inevitably the curves crossed such that there were more fishermen than fish to support them, and US conservationists began to advocate for catch and release here as well.

An early proponent was Lee Wulff, the fishing icon, who in 1938 wrote, "A good gamefish is too valuable to be caught only once." How concisely the laconic Wulff captures our philosophy.

Bernard "Lefty" Kreh, the great southpaw caster and one of the best-known fishing guides, was also a big proponent, including saltwater fish. He advocated for catch and release among fellow guides in South Florida, where he resided in the 1960s. Through research, Lefty demonstrated that the fish his clients were catching had been getting smaller over time. Eventually he was able to convince many guides that, in the long run, catch and release would be better for business. Explaining this to people, Lefty was known to quip, "Do you cook up your golf balls after playing golf?" Kreh turned ninety this year and is still a vocal catch-and-release advocate.

Kreh and many others have written how-to guidelines. Fish are delicate and don't do well out of water. Releasing one in an unhealthy state is hardly more effective than shoot and release, which, obviously, has never caught on with hunters. So, the guidelines are all about keeping fish healthy and uninjured. It starts with not playing the fish to the point of exhaustion. Actually it starts with selecting tippet that's strong enough to allow you to haul a resisting the fish in without breaking. Ideally, the fish never comes out of the water and you are able to remove the hook quickly.

Fly-fishing inherently lends itself to catch and release as it utilizes a single hook. Generally, the fly hook pierces only the trout's cartilaginous lip, so the hook comes right out with no harm done. But sometimes an enthusiastic trout will get hooked a little too well. Most of us use a hemostat or small pliers to rotate the hook point out. Barbless hooks are required in some waters, and bending down the barb makes for easier removal. We also use special nets that are fairly soft, fine meshed, and forgiving, so that fish aren't injured by the net.

When removing fish from the water or the net, we wet our hands to go easier on the mucus coating that protects the fish (trout are a little slimy). Finally, when the fish is tired, it's good practice to hold it gently facing upstream to "catch its breath" until it squirms loose and scoots away.

———

Not all frequenters of the Grant subscribe to the catch-and-release philosophy, including a certain professor we run into from time to time. Phil likes to tell it this way:

At Hellgate now and then, I run into one of my favorite Dartmouth professors. At the end of his extremely popular freshman history seminar, he told me, "Well, you're no genius, but I think you'll get through Dartmouth." How's that for a vote of confidence?

The guy is a character—an alum, born and raised in a Maine mill town and you couldn't miss it in his accent. It's not way out on a limb to say the guy knows more about his field than anyone on the planet and is an extraordinary storyteller.

Thus, it was a delight to bump into my old prof that first time in the pools just above Hellgate Gorge. He was kind enough to feign remembering me. Evidently he and his wife (who always seemed to be back at the cabin cooking) had been regulars at the Grant for decades. They liked the fishing around Hellgate, but his practical streak kept him on the road side of the river in the Gorge Cabin, where our group has yet to stay. We talked about getting together for drinks, though that never happened. Still, it was always nice to see him on the river and chat him up briefly, which seemed to happen every couple of years.

Here's the thing about the good professor: He's a worm fisherman and has no use for the idea of catch and release. He uses a rig like you've never seen. A fly rod with some kind of attractor, a fly I think, below which hangs a 6- or 12-inch leader weighted down with some split shot (lead, of course) and a hook with a live worm. Typically, he uses the length of the rod to dip the bait into various likely holes at the head of pools, below little falls, and along a foam line. Sometimes, though, I saw him bumble the worm along the bottom, using a technique not unlike nymphing.

And, he would slay them. And I do mean slay. On a day when The Boys were having moderate luck, I recall him pulling a string of trout out of a stream-side pool where he was keeping them cold. There must have been six or eight, all more than ten inches, very unusual that far upstream.

In all our years of going to the Grant, I'll bet that, collectively, the seven of us Boys have kept fewer than a dozen fish. Total. We even feel funny having barbs on our fly hooks. How seemingly incongruous that a highly educated, supremely thoughtful nature lover like the good professor would have such apparent disregard for the tragedy of the fishing commons, especially in this unstocked, wild trout water. Okay, we wouldn't object to keeping a few, but it's been years since "catching your limit" was an admirable goal.

I know I sound elitist when I say, "You can take the boy out of the North Woods, but . . ." But I believe *he* is actually the elitist, of the Maine woods kind. He, at least implicitly, must feel that because he grew up fishing this way, it remains his right to continue to do so. It's no business of the invading flatlanders, the cause of all that fishing pressure anyway (*by Gawd*), to tell him what should or shouldn't be on the end of his line. He's that kind of guy.

I wish he'd do differently, but I actually buy the squatter's-rights argument. It's a disposition I share, one that prompts me to disregard the decade-old one-way sign on Sea Street in Cotuit, the little village on Cape Cod where I spend much of my time. I grew up traveling from Main Street to Oceanview by way of Sea Street, and I will continue to travel that way (*Gawdammit*) even though a one-way sign now points in the other direction. At least my old professor isn't breaking the law.

––––––

But The Boys are all about catch and release and have a great rule to facilitate the practice: If we bring a fish within a rod's length and it spits the hook, we can consider it caught and released. We call it a long distance release, or LDR.

One of us: "How did you do, Bob?"

Bob: "Well, I hooked and lost a nice one, landed two about ten inches, and had a couple LDRs, both thirteen or fourteen inches."

Statistically speaking, fish that are long distance released are about 2.5 inches longer than those we get to see up close. Go figure.

We also have a term for when the fish hits your fly but you miss the hook-up altogether. We call it low-impact fishing. When the fish are falling short of even hitting your fly, we call that "unproductive waters." There are days when we go really easy on the trout population, especially Klingon.

To discourage their keeping smaller fish, we tell our occasional male guests another of our rules: "You can only keep fish that are bigger than your pecker." It is entertaining to see the look on their faces while they try to decide whether this is a good thing or a bad thing.

Today, organizations ranging from the National Park Service to

Trout Unlimited strongly encourage catch and release. A Park Service brochure says:

> Catch and release fishing improves native fish populations by allowing more fish to remain and reproduce in the ecosystem. This practice provides an opportunity for increasing numbers of anglers to enjoy fishing and to successfully catch fish. Releasing all native fish caught while in a national park ensures that enjoyment of this recreational opportunity will last for generations to come.

The Boys agree, but we recognize that there are different strategies for managing fishing waters that may be under more or less fishing pressure from the masses. Waters closer to population centers are heavily stocked with hatchery trout in what are called "put and take" fisheries—the idea being that many people do, in fact, want to catch their limit for the table or freezer. Essentially, instead of delivering to the store, a state hatchery delivers them to the local stream. In rural New England, where incomes are low and jobs are scarce, the local population may rely on fish, venison, and wild turkey to help feed the family. It's a good way to accommodate the consumptive fishing pressure, thereby relieving the pressure in wilder places, like the Grant.

Some lakes and rivers, believe it or not, may be over-stocked with certain species or size classes of game fish. Fishery managers may encourage anglers to take and keep some species to benefit others (e.g. taking lake trout from Maine's Sebago Lake to help the salmon population), or may have a "slot limit" that allows anglers to keep only a certain size (say, six to nine inches) while releasing the rest to allow the larger fish to grow even bigger.

In most of the Grant, catch and release is voluntary, as a 2012 brochure published by the College explains:

> The following provisions are voluntary at this time. Persons fishing in the Grant are strongly encouraged to:
>
> A. Practice "catch and release" of all trout and salmon.
> B. If you keep fish, follow a voluntary two fish per person per day limit.
> C. Use single barbless hooks on all flies, lures, or bait hooks.
>
> Only the waters in the southern part of the Grant are regulated as catch and release, artificial lures only:

From the confluence of the Dead Diamond and Magalloway River near the southerly end of the airstrip, upstream to the confluence of the Swift Diamond and Dead Diamond rivers near Peaks Cabin, and on that portion of the Magalloway located in New Hampshire upstream of its confluence with the Dead Diamond, only single barbless-hook lures or flies may be used. No worms or bait are allowed. All trout must be released unharmed.

In Lamb Valley Brook, Loomis Valley Brook, and Alder Brook, wild trout regulations apply. Only single barbless-hook lures or flies may be used. No worms or bait are allowed. All trout must be released unharmed. These waters are open to fishing January 1 to Labor Day only.

It's always bugged and bewildered us that the proverbial "they" don't just make all the waters of the Grant compulsory catch and release or, better, fly-fishing only. Why not? Perhaps revealing our elitist prejudice, we have been inclined to speculate that this is a consequence of the Great Unwashed, less forward thinking than we are, pressing the College to maintain the status quo.

Not so, it turns out. According to the master plan for the Grant, the College feels that more restrictions could actually be worse for the fish population. The argument is that the rivers and fish are technically public resources, so stricter regulations would require public hearings that would draw unwanted attention to the wild fishery. Furthermore, officially designated catch-and-release waters must be marked as such on maps of the area and therefore might act as a bulls-eye for clever fishermen. The College calculates that the lesser evil is to keep the waters on a daily limit while educating visitors and encouraging conservation practices. This also allows visitors who want to enjoy a trout dinner, after traveling all this way, to do so at their discretion. As we've told our kids, everything is okay in moderation.

There is one, very exclusive group of fish that must be released everywhere in the Grant. Fish tagged and equipped with antennae must be returned to the water and fishermen are asked to report the catch to New Hampshire Fish and Game. Although we have never caught one of these high-tech trout, we have had some interesting encounters with wildlife biologists conducting fascinating studies. One woman we spoke with, who was operating a radio receiver above the Gorge, excited us with the discovery that there was a twenty-inch trout downstream, within a hundred feet. None of us has ever caught a twenty-inch trout in the Grant. The radio researchers have discovered that the trout of the Grant are much rangier than they had believed. Some tagged fish regularly head to the Magalloway, Rapid, and Androscoggin rivers in the low-water warmer months and come back in the fall.

Whatever the regulations, The Boys will continue to release as many fish as we can. The more we release, the happier we are. And why eat fresh sautéed trout when there's Veg-All?

We like to think that on occasion we encounter fish we've met in the past and released as manifestations of Lee Wulff's chestnut about the value of a game fish. Guy puts it another way: "I like watching them swim away as much I like catching them."

We all do.

Art & Lit in the Grant

By Bob Chamberlin

> Many remedies are suggested for the avoidance
> of worry and mental overstrain by persons who, over
> prolonged periods, have to bear exceptional responsibilities
> and discharge duties upon a very large scale.
> —Winston Churchill, *Painting as a Pastime*

My wife had given me a small set of watercolors, which I took out every August on our annual vacation to the Maine coast. Growing up, I spent much more time on the baseball diamond than in art classes, but I found joy in capturing my views of Maine by swishing paint onto thick, textured paper. I brought my kit along on my first Grant trip and have done so ever since, occasionally during the weekends exchanging my rod and fly box for a brush and paint box. My first paintings are not memorable, except for the fact that they were painted on postcard-size watercolor paper, all the better to finish a painting in one short sitting on a rock at stream side. I still have a few from those early seasons. Arranging them sequentially, I'm pleased to report, shows clear improvement over the years.

I specifically recall a day when we were fishing the upper Dead. The sun was very bright, and I had had enough fishing for a spell, so I brought out my watercolor paraphernalia, which I kept stored in a Ziploc bag in a compartment of my fishing vest. I was just getting started when Billy walked up from the river. Absorbing and appreciating the scene, he exclaimed, "How sublime!" I will always remember that moment and those words. It *was* sublime, and I was doing my best to capture that sense in my artwork.

One of the great things about painting is the way that looking at one's own work can help you recall all the sensations you experienced while creating it. Years later, when I look at one of my paintings light, weather, sounds, and location all come back vividly.

Staying at Sam's Cabin recently, I noticed that an old watercolor I had painted, "Leaping Trout," still remained push-pinned to the cork board. After many years, the painting has become as much a part of the place as the cribbage board and the visitor's journal.

————

One year at Sam's Cabin, Billy, our resident English major and Renaissance man, pulled out Robert Frost's "Witch of Coos." (See pages 184–188) Noting that the Grant is in the northern half of Coos County (pronounced *KO-ahs*), Bill read the eerie poem aloud after dinner one evening. Once he finished, we passed the book around, reflecting on specific passages and debating what Frost had likely wanted us to take away. The scene of our discussion went something like this:

Guy: Where did that all come from? Sounds like poor Frost had a bad dream, maybe after eating something like tonight's chili. [*He belches.*]

Phil: He never graduated from Dartmouth, you know. Dropped out.

Billy: Admit it, Guy, it's a great poem. One of my favorites. Much more there than meets the ear. I don't think it's a bad dream. It's a bizarre, macabre story about infidelity, murder, and isolation—and it's hilarious!

Guy: Yeah, nothing like bones crawling up from the basement to the attic to give me a good chuckle. You know, before we moved to New Gloucester our old house in Buxton actually had a dirt floor in the basement. Very well could have been bones buried down there. I gotta say, it creeps me out.

Billy: Tell me you can read the line "I had a vision of him mounted for this walk not like a man but like a chandelier" and not crack up. Or "it carried itself like a pile of dishes." Nothing like absurd juxtaposition to get me going.

Phil: English majors.

Norm: I love the image of the woman looking through the button box for the finger bones. It's brilliant. Hearing that line I felt like I was right in her kitchen. English majors rule, Philip; engineers drool. And while I have the floor, I will also note that Frost condenses the entire story into just two lines, when the Mother, referring to the bones, tells the visitor:

"They were a man's his father killed for me. / I mean a man he killed instead of me."

Phil: Let me see that book. [*He flips the page*] How 'bout when the son says: "It's harmless. Mother hears it in the night / Halting perplexed behind the barrier / Of door and headboard. Where it wants to get / Is back into the cellar where it came from."

Billy [*laughing, spittle flying*]: And the Mother says: "We'll never let them, will we, son! We'll never!"

Bob: I like the part where the mother mentions the Indian and says, "He said the dead had souls," and then she mentions how suspicious she is of the dead because "there's something the dead are keeping back." Not sure what to make of that exchange, but I like it.

Billy: His genius is that he manages to do two radically different things at once—he tells a really dark, depressing New England tale and spices it with such piquant asides that it simultaneously reads as comedy. I guess I'm a sucker for dark comedy. This is definitely one of Frost's best.

————

Since "The Witch," readings have become a tradition on our weekends at the Grant, and several of us have brought along pieces to share with the group. One, a short passage from a Bailey White story called "An Interesting Life," which I first heard on National Public Radio, I recited aloud for its imagery:

> One night a steward woke her up and told her the captain wanted her to come to the bridge at once. He had something he wanted to show her. She hurried up and stood by him at the rail.
> And there she saw the most exciting thing one can see while on board a ship at sea—another ship. The night was dark, and the only sound was the lapping of the waves. She does not remember whether it was warm or cold—only the sight of that magnificent ship, lit up from bow to stern, silently gliding past in the night. The silence, the blackness of the water, and the remoteness of the passing ship made her think in great depth of the mysteries of things she did not know. The captain's voice startled her when he finally spoke:
> "Take a good look, my child. You are seeing history in the

making, for that ship is no ordinary one, but the greatest ship ever built. It is the RMS Titanic on her maiden voyage."

—From *Mama Makes Up Her Mind: And Other Dangers of Southern Living* (1993)

Another popular one was "My Symphony" by William Ellery Channing, a contemporary of Emerson and Thoreau.

To live content with small means,
To seek elegance rather than luxury,
And refinement rather than fashion,
To be worthy, not respectable, and wealthy, not rich,
To study hard, think quietly, talk gently, act frankly,
To listen to stars and birds, babes and sages, with open heart,
To bear all cheerfully,
Do all bravely,
Await occasions,
Hurry never—
In a word, to let the spiritual, unbidden and unconscious, grow up through the common.
This is to be my symphony.

After which, I remember, one of The Boys recalled an adage of unknown origin about the requirements of a "Man of the 80s": A good kisser, only macho in emergencies, and able to commit. It's a standard to which all good men of any decade might aspire.

And finally another favorite reading, a classic:

Testament of a Fisherman
By Robert Traver (pen name of John Voelker)

I fish because I love to; because I love the environs where trout are found, which are invariably beautiful and I hate the environs where crowds of people are found, which are invariably ugly;

because of all the television commercials, cocktail parties, and assorted social posturing I thus escape;

because, in a world where most men seem to spend their lives doing things they hate, my fishing is at once an endless source of delight and an act of small rebellion;

because trout do not lie or cheat and cannot be bought or bribed or impressed by power, but respond only to quietude and humility and endless patience;

because I suspect that men are going along this way for the last time, and I for one don't want to waste the trip;

because only in the woods can I find solitude without loneliness;

because bourbon out of an old tin cup always tastes better out there;

because maybe one day I will catch a mermaid;

and, finally, not because I regard fishing as being so terribly important but because I suspect that so many of the other concerns of men are equally unimportant - and not nearly so much fun.

Permission granted by Kitchie Hill, Inc.

Phil loves the line about bourbon.

A few years ago, I acquired an antique letterpress printing press, so I decided to hand-print copies of another favorite reading, a passage from Izaak Walton's *The Compleat Angler*, which I gave out to The Boys. A reproduction of my print is the frontispiece of this book.

––––––––

Along with the readings, several of us have continued to paint on our weekends at the Grant. Phil often brings his set, and DVW, as I refer to Guy because I missed the undergraduate indoctrination to his rugby and fraternity nickname, sometimes brings his. Phil is accomplished at enhancing his watercolors with pen and ink. In recent years, DVW has shifted to photography which he posts to his website.

In 2012, on our last day in the Grant, I took DVW's digital camera and snapped about a hundred shots of my friends fishing, and DVW dutifully posted those photos to his website a few days after the trip. I selected what I considered to be the best of each angler, in terms of light, gesture, and composition, for a set of watercolor paintings to gift the upcoming holiday season. Luckily, I had also arranged to take my first real watercolor workshop with Don Andrews, a nationally known watercolor artist and instructor, that September. Don has a particular wet-on-wet style that gives a lot of life to his paintings, and which can be employed for watercolor paintings of fly-fishing, and I wanted to practice that style. Some of the results appear in the color section of this book.

I would be remiss if, in a chapter concerning art, I neglected to recognize Guy's artistry in tying flies. The products of his efforts are works of great beauty as well as valued additions to each of our fly boxes. Most years he runs mini-clinics, talking several of us through the intricate process of producing different fly patterns, but none of us has picked up the skill or inclinations of the master.

———

So, yes, the liberal arts are alive and well at the Grant. What started as simply a fishing trip has tapped into our wider talents and interests. Beyond painting and reading, beyond the science and physics of fly-fishing, we also explore and encourage our mutual appreciation for art, literature, music, philosophy, and even politics. Walk into the cabin during cocktail hour, and you might think you'd stumbled upon a backwoods book club, as Billy, Norm, and Phil delve into recent novels by their favorite authors.

Last Christmas, I sent each of The Boys a copy of *Stumbling on Happiness* by Daniel Gilbert. As Gilbert notes, three primary choices drive our ability to find happiness: where we live, what we do, and with whom we do it. And so it is at the Grant, where, for the weekend at least, these choices are self-evident. And happiness ensues.

The Year of The Kids

By Phil Odence

From the outset of our weekends in the woods there was an unwritten rule: no girls, no kids. One year, however, extreme circumstances brought my family along with me to the Grant.

I was working in Hanover, traveling a lot, and was scheduled on a red eye to Europe for two weeks on the Sunday of our fishing weekend. So, my plan was to head up Thursday morning and get back early Saturday to give me some time with the family before disappearing for a fortnight. The spanner in the works was that the office required my brief presence Friday morning. Arriving at the Grant on Friday afternoon and scooting Saturday morning didn't make sense, so my outside-the-box solution was to bring the mountain to Mohammad and cart my gang up to the Grant. My gracious, understanding compadres acceded, especially when I told them I'd lined up the nearby Fish & Game Cabin for the Odences.

Later to be moved, rebuilt, and renamed as Pete Blodgett Cabin (in 2002), Fish & Game, at the time, was a hundred yards or so east of the Hellgate Hilton, in the field below the swimming hole. Close enough, but far enough. In previous years, we'd noticed the structure, though had never seen anyone stay there. When I'd dialed the Outdoor Programs Office a few days before, I was delighted to find that the cabin was available and even more delighted when the sometimes brusque administrator told me she wouldn't charge me. She did mention that although occasionally folks stayed there, it lacked some of the amenities of other cabins and was in a bit of disrepair. Someone more attuned to subtle clues might have been more inclined to look a gift horse in the mouth. But, hey, it was available, it was near the Hellgate Hilton and The Boys, and it would neatly resolve my predicament.

———

The weather was picture perfect when we arrived at the Grant and forded the Dead. Bookie (age nine), Charlotte (seven), and the dogs, Trouser and Hallie, ran ahead as Beth and I carted gear across the field. My Outdoor Programs contact proved to be the master of understatement when she'd alluded to a lack of amenities. The first thing we did after opening the door was to tip a couple of chairs on their sides to barricade the kitchen so the aforementioned kids and dogs would not slip into the truck-tire-sized chasm in the floor. A couple of half-inch plywood sheets masked what we presumed were a couple of similar gaps in the living room floor. Beth, being a great sport, played along.

Things looked up from there. It was an unusually hot afternoon, which made for great swimming in Hellgate pool. And The Boys of the Grant were most accommodating that night, feeding us a delightful dinner. My gang flashlighted back to F & G while I stayed to carouse for a bit. Later I joined them and achieved a solid night's sleep. The girls were up with the sun, and we let Mom sleep in while we took the dogs and bounded up to the Hilton for coffee.

Events began to unravel when Beth, not a big fan of backwoods fauna, awoke nose to nose with a large mouse on her chest. Soon she was running up to the Hilton, vowing never to go back to the cabin. A number of the crew were leaving that night, so the remaining Boys—as I recall, it was just Guy and his brother Doug, who was with us in the early years—invited us to move in.

We got Bookie outfitted for some fishing that morning above Hellgate. Beth and Charlotte came along to spectate, but by midmorning the black flies got the better of them and they headed back to the Hellgate Hilton. En route, they spotted a bear across the field and opted for a safer view from inside the cabin. There they settled in for a card game and reading on the bunk.

Meanwhile, in the smaller water north of Hellgate Gorge, Bookie was thrashing away at one pool for more than an hour. She'd gotten a hit or two early on, enough to make her declare that she would not leave that hole until she extracted that fish. Guy and I tried to explain about letting the pool rest, but she was relentless, standing on a rock in her running shoes, warm-up pants, turtleneck, and baseball hat. It's probably the photo of her with the nine-inch trout that I remember, not the actual incident, but, yes, she caught it. Finally, somehow, the fish must have gotten fed up and just said, "Screw it, I'll bite." Perhaps the most excited Bookie had ever been was the moment she hooked that "whopper," as she called it. I shuffled over as quickly as my waders would allow and helped her land it. The day was a great success.

Phil's daughter Bookie lands "a whopper" with Phil manning the net during the Year of the Kids. Photo by Doug Van Wie.

———

We returned to the Hilton, excited to relate Bookie's epic success, only to find Beth, Charlotte, Hallie, and Trouser on the porch of the cabin where they'd been for about two hours. Two hours and three seconds earlier, they'd encountered two broom-handle-length snakes cohabitating the cabin with them. Evidently, that put them over their limit for wildlife in one day. So, bear sighting notwithstanding, they'd remained on the open porch swatting countless bugs until our return.

Doug, a natural naturalist, hearing the snake report, proceeded directly to the fridge, correctly surmising that the reptiles were likely attracted to the warmth of the propane flame that powered it. He reached in behind and came away with a handful of three good-sized snakes, all squirming and writhing.

Those reptilian squatters having been relocated to deep in the woods, the girls were grudgingly willing to re-enter the cabin, but only temporarily. This was to be Beth's last trip to the Grant, and probably Charlotte's. Weeks later, when I returned from Europe, the dogs were just getting off the medication they'd been taking to reduce the swelling from the mass of black fly bites around their necks, hidden beneath their thick fur. The girls had stopped itching, too.

Bookie returned to the Grant with me and Guy for a winter excursion in early 2014. It would not surprise me to see her back at her pool one day, pursuing a descendent of her first trout.

Years later, we found the Hellgate Hilton cabin log entry from the Year of the Kids, dated June 11 – 13, 1999. Guy's summary of our trip concluded this way: "Beth decided we should reinstitute the no-girl rule. (Actually there is no such rule, but she wants an excuse to stay home next time.)"

The Hag Trout of Coos County

By Norm Richter

T he Boys don't believe me. Can you imagine? They don't believe I was swept down through the Gorge and lived to tell. We'd been fishing at the Confluence of the Swift and the Dead on a late afternoon. The sunlight made the river look like wrinkled tin foil. I lost sight of The Boys as I worked my way around a bend to the head of the Gorge—a place of mystic significance for me because here I once pulled a sixteen-inch brook trout out of the first deep pool. (I don't think they believed that story either.) After a wide, flat stretch with gentle runs, the river funnels between two high walls of granite with dark green spruce and cedar hanging down like mermaid hair from both sides. The current runs white and hot here, plunging down, down, down through a series of frothy pools for as far as you can see.

Well, I hooked a fish, a thrill running up my arm, but it was more than I could handle. There I was, balancing with one leg on an outcropping of rock, trying to angle my retrieve along the far glide, when a giant grabbed my line and yanked. The next instant, I was unmoored, sliding into the current. My waders filled with what felt like ice water in seconds, and I was dragged under. I tumbled a ways, clinging to my rod, and then the current pinned me briefly against a shale ledge beneath the surface. I opened my eyes. For a few long seconds, I stared through the swirl of bubbles into a dark space under the ledge. Something moved, coming out of the black. A trout, but not just any trout. No, this could only be the Hag Trout of Coos County.

Some may not have heard of the Hag Trout. Hard to imagine, but perhaps they went off for a term to UC San Diego during sophomore year, met a surfer girl, and never returned. The rest of us know. The Hag Trout was made famous by Thoreau, in his poem of the same name. Later, a Mr. Frost added his own contribution to the legends of

Coos (more on that later), but for those who cannot recall the original, it begins:

> I stayed the night for shelter at a cabin
> Behind the mountains, with a fisherman and son,
> Two old-believers. They did all the talking.
> FISHERMAN: Let me
> Tell you what a Hanover Indian once told me,
> As we fished and I had one on.
> He said the trout were souls, but when I asked him
> How could that be— I thought the trout were sport,
> The fish broke my line. Don't that make you suspicious
> That there's something the trout are keeping back?
> Yes, there's something the trout are keeping back.
> SON: You wouldn't want to tell him what we have
> Up attic, father?
> FISHERMAN: A fly rod—or more to point, the bones of one.
> (Where did I see one of those pieces lately?
> Son, hand me my fly box—it must be there.)
> SON: But the headboard of father's bed is pushed
> Against the' attic door: the door is nailed.
> It's harmless. Father hears it in the night
> Moving perplexed behind the barrier
> Of door and headboard. Where it wants to get
> Is back into the river where it became bewitched.
> FISHERMAN: We'll never let it, will we, son! We'll never!
> SON: It fished the river forty years ago,
> In whose hands is not important
> (Though he sits there across the table),
> It hooked a small brookie,
> Which in turn was snatched by a bigger trout,
> Which was gobbled a moment later,
> By a Trout of no earthly provenance…

It goes on, but you know it, of course. The point is this was the creature I knew I now faced in the frothing gorge. Her mouth and bulk was more grouper than trout, and she held me with her glittering eye. For that long moment, the Hag Trout had my will.

She broke my trance when she loomed forth out of the dark, big as a manatee. With a casual flick of her fluke, she cast me to the surface, leaving me gasping on the ledge above the waterfall. I lay down my rod and quickly unbuckled my bloated waders, letting them fall away.

I took up my rod again, wondering where the line went, when the water of the pool boiled and erupted. The Hag Trout rose like a geyser, her tail flicking at the cedars, raining broken branches down upon me. Her arc took her over my head and down into the next pool. Then I saw my line, glinting in the afternoon sun, trailing from her monstrous mouth. In the next instant, my arms nearly yanked from their sockets, I was pulled forward like a skipping stone.

It was a wonder the line did not break. I do tie a wicked strong nail knot, but more likely it was bewitched. I surfed across the lower pool, my stomach on a broken cedar bough. Then again the Hag Trout breached skyward, casually gulping a circling osprey before plunging into the next lower pool. I was dragged over another rock ledge and skittered along like bedraggled pondweed. Again and again, pool after pool, I descended the gorge, the cedar surfboard disintegrating beneath me.

The moose was unexpected. He stood in one of the wide lower pools, water up to his belly. His head, crowned with antlers, came up slowly as the Hag Trout sailed over and split the water beyond like Moses. The moose peered dimly at the whirlpool the Hag Trout had left behind, just as I came skidding in from his blind side, riding the last of the cedar bough. My fading momentum was just enough to deposit me on his back, wouldn't you know. Finally, the leader line snapped, and followed the Hag Trout into the black depths.

You might think this would have spooked the moose. And, yes, it surely did. You might think this would have launched me on a wild ride through the forest, white knuckles gripping the antlers like the handlebars of a Harley. Yes again. But the ride was remarkably short-lived, because of the bear.

She reared suddenly out of the brush and took a mighty swipe at the moose, leaving bloody claw stripes along his side. He pulled up short (no appetite for argument with a she-bear), turned abruptly, and backtracked to the river fast. Behind us, I could hear the undergrowth snap and crack; the bear pursued with thudding strides.

At the river's edge, the moose did not stop. He plunged directly into the wide pool, to swim across. Lacking any plan, I hung on. Behind us, I heard the bear hit the water at full gallop. The moose, tired of my weight, swung his great antlers back and forth to shake me off.

I tumbled into the cold water and struck out swimming for the rocks below the waterfall.

The bear suddenly bellowed, more enraged, if that were possible. I pulled myself up on a boulder, and saw the Hag Trout rise up with her gaping mouth streaming river water. It closed on the bear's lower body, but could not manage the rest. The bear twisted around and began to slash at the fish with its tungsten claws. Great gouges appeared along the Hag Trout's scales. The river froth roiled red. The Hag Trout swung her massive tail around and struck the bear's head, first on one side and then the other. At each blow, the surrounding forest shuddered and rotted trees toppled. It was too much for the she-bear. Her counter-blows weakened. Slowly, slowly, the Hag Trout dragged the beast below the surface.

Now, all this you can readily accept as part of nature's drama, so I hesitate to relate how strangely this adventure concluded. To understand, you must return to Mr. Frost and his story of Coos County.

You will recall his tale ends with a man's bones still upstairs in the house of Toffile Barre. But Sam, the caretaker of the Grant (whose grandfather knew Toffile's family), once told me how the weird tale played out:

> After the traveler left, the son pulled away the headboard and went up attic. He chased the bones among the cobwebs, mowing the room at the level of his knees until they lay across the floor like broken dishes. He collected the pieces in a burlap sack. It sat ill with him, that the truth had been told to a stranger. No good could come of the bones remaining there. The son rode to Wentworth's Location, hiked a ways into the Second College Grant, and scattered the bones into the pool at the top of the Gorge. He said he watched the current carry the white pieces over the rocks and downstream.

This all came back to me as I sat there trying to sort out what I had just witnessed. Evidently the commotion in the pool caused by the death struggle between the she-bear and the Hag Trout had been too much for the spectral skeleton Sam had spoken of, for suddenly something very peculiar took place. The water stirred by my feet, and a skeletal hand rose out of the water, and found purchase on a ridge of rock near the boulder on which I rested. The bones pulled themselves up to sit beside me, balancing with emotion. (A tongue of fire flashed out and licked along his upper teeth. Smoke rolled inside the sockets of his eyes.) We sat a while, companionably, watching the riffles swirl, the last of the blood draining away downstream. I thought to offer him my rod to hold, as a comfort, but his fingers struck me as too brittle to manage it. After a time, the last of the evening light faded. The churning of the water subsided. He turned his hollow eyes to me, and, holding my gaze, somewhat sadly I thought, he let himself slide back into the deep from whence he had come.

Thinking on the Fly

By Phil Odence and The Boys

Boys like to talk about sports. And sometimes sports talk drifts from last night's game into Imagine This. What if Bobby Orr hadn't gotten hurt? What if Ted Williams was playing today? What if you could draft a rugby team of NFL players?

The Boys of the Grant talk about all kinds of stuff, sometimes even fishing. Our version of the "What if" question: What if you could take only *one* fly into the Grant?

We've been at this fishing business for a lot of years, and everyone has developed strong opinions about the right flies to use at various times. We've often pondered the One Fly question. Below, each of The Boys contributes a response to the question. This was a blind exercise; no one read the others' contributions before penning his own. At the end of the chapter, I provide the correct answer. Photos of the most common flies mentioned are shown in the color pages.

———

First, Bob's well-reasoned, albeit misguided, thinking:

I recall a religious moment, when, in the process of cleaning and organizing my flies on the Merrill Brook Cabin dining table, I found myself creating two groups. Group One consisted of the workhorse flies commonly used on our June trips: Hornberg, Woolly Bugger, Elk Hair Caddis, Adams Dry, Hare's Ear Nymph, Wood Special, Muddler Minnow. In Group Two was everything else.

L.L. Bean has the Guide's Choice Selection, the Deluxe Eastern Selection, and the Life Cycle Fly Selection. Orvis has a Must-Have Selection (Adams Parachute, Elkwing Caddis, Copper John Nymphs, Woolly Buggers), the Eastern Trout Summer Selection, and its version of the Life Cycle Selection.

I call my personal Group One the "Grant Selection," and I can offer a simple introduction to each fly in this stellar collection:

The **Hornberg**, our number-one starter fly, with its dry-to-wet resiliency.

The **Woolly Bugger** with its track record for larger trout.

The **Elk Hair Caddis**, with its remarkable buoyancy, enabling weakening eyes to track its drift.

The **Hare's Ear Nymph**, which, for me, is a decent standby that never fails to irritate Phil when I catch fish with it.

The **Wood Special**, introduced to our fly boxes by DVW, who has tied dozens over the years.

And, finally, the **Muddler Minnow**. This is my choice. Low water or high, hot or cool, clear or overcast. I like the lighter colors for tracking. I like the moderate-to-small sizes (hook sizes 8 – 12) to increase the size range of fish that can be attracted.

For years I had heard this was an effective fly, but was regularly shut out when I tried it. I didn't understand how or whether to get it down in the water; how or whether to let it drift; or how to work it as the line bent in the stream. It turns out, any number of techniques might be employed. All of them eluded me. Until one year...

Fishing the joint waters by the Bridge I had, in error (but, really, do we ever do things "in error," especially when pursuing trout?), clumsily jerked a Muddler through high waves, angling the fly upstream to downstream. On this particular cast and retrieve I noticed two largish fish jumping at the fly, as if in irritation. I repeated the motion in the same place on the next cast and caught a fat, colorful brook trout. Thus was established a technique I used the rest of that evening, catching ten more wonderful fat fish. I have continued to use this gambit year after year (with more modest success than that first evening, to be honest).

My devotion to the Muddler was sealed some years later. DVW and I were the last ones to pack up and head home and decided to wade above the Bridge on our way out. We positioned ourselves about 100 feet apart and, after a few minutes Dave exclaimed, "A smelt run!"

We saw silver flashes all around us, some from predator and some from prey. Though I'd heard of these conditions from other fishermen, in other places and times, I had never found myself in this situation:

landed fish were stuffed with long silver smelts, tails sticking out of each trout's mouth, some of which were attached to still living smelts. We could, if we were so inclined, pull a smelt out of the trout's digestive tract by its tail, but there was something more important to do—get my line out there!

The Muddler Minnow seemed to be the ideal choice for that situation and many, many others since. I am extremely grateful to it.

————

Klingon's twist:

First off, fishing in the Grant is hard. As perhaps the only member of our intrepid group who has done little fly-fishing outside of the annual Grant trip, I suffered for years thinking that this was simply what fly-fishing *is*. You make a couple of hundred casts, and then you might hook a six- or nine-inch brook trout.

My perception of fly-fishing changed on a trip to Alaska last summer. We spent nine days in southeastern Alaska exploring the Inside Passage (spectacular!), but I felt that I needed to explore fishing while there, so my wife, Dana, and I added a slight (1,000 miles) detour from Ketchikan to Anchorage in order to fish the Kenai Peninsula. This would be my first time fly-fishing with a professional guide. No need to struggle with my poor eyesight and poorer fine motor skills: I had heard that the guide actually ties the flies on for you!

After a strenuous hike with our guide "Fly Bob," we found ourselves at the Russian River. Now, Fly Bob clearly knew how to fish, but he wasn't so mobile. And he looked to be about ninety. At some point in his life Bob had broken his ankle and apparently took care of it himself, given the long distance to adequate health care. I was sure we were going to have to carry him back out, so I kept on the lookout for ways to get him up to the trailhead once he passed on.

In any event, Fly Bob was going to have to spend almost all of his time assisting Dana, as this was her first attempt at fly-fishing. His lack of attention to me did not impact my experience, however, as this style of fly-fishing didn't require changing flies. We were there during the sockeye salmon spawn, and were fishing for Dolly Varden trout, who were feasting on the salmon eggs. The salmon were so thick that you had to wade into them and try not to step on them. Since the trout were eating eggs, the fly was simply a pink bead on a hook. I never had to change it once and caught over thirty trout, every one bigger than the biggest I had ever caught in the Grant. All you have to do is travel to Alaska when the salmon are spawning and you won't have to worry about choosing a fly.

Back to the topic of this chapter, my aforementioned optical and motor-skill limitations have prevented me from mastering the quick switch of flies, so I am generally content to cast for long periods with 1) whatever fly has successfully hooked a trout for me that day (or the previous day), or 2) whatever fly was the response when I called over to one of my mates asking what fly had he used that resulted in the nice trout I just saw him lift from the stream. I am partial to dry flies, owing to the aesthetic pleasure of seeing a trout rise to take a fly on the surface. Since I spend so little time actually catching fish, I enjoy watching the journey of a dry fly traveling down a riffle. So, my choice for my one fly would be either an Elk Hair Caddis or a Hornberg. I doubt one would catch me more fish than the other.

———

Norm makes a good case:

I never much cared for deep-water fishing, where the boat does the fishing for you. Especially when there's a guide who rigs everything, decides where to go, and then hands you the rod to reel in while offering advice mostly intended to prevent you from damaging his equipment. No, I like fishing on the surface, where you can read the action of the insects or the birds, see the flash of silver as the fish come to check out what you're offering, and see the water boil as they take the lure.

You *can* get that from a boat, and I often enjoy fishing on the waters of the Narragansett Bay or off Block Island, chasing striped bass and blues. But the best is on a stream, surrounded by tall pines, standing in cold water that rushes by up to your knees; where rocks and sharp bends in the riverbed break up the flow and create infinitely varying pockets of water that may or may not hold trout; and where, if you are right, the trout will rise up out of the water in their ferocity to inhale your fly.

I like it so much that I'm the worse fisherman for it. I'll choose the fly I *want to fish with* instead of the fly that will actually catch the fish. I scold myself that I should be nymphing in this pool or should be putting on sinking line to get down deep. But, no, I just don't want to more often than not. I'd rather watch the fly drift the perfect dead drift, even if it passes untouched over the heads of big trout holding down low. I'll play the poorer probability that one of these will go against pattern and surge up to take my fly so I'll get to see its shadow move up against the submerged stones, see the hard take and the water churn, and have sight and touch align perfectly as my rod tip bends over.

So if I were asked to choose only one fly to fish the Grant, you see where this has to go. Not a nymph, or a Woolly Bugger, or even a streamer. A Hornberg is good and serves the purpose, and what's not to love about that reliable fly? But there is nothing quite like a dry fly that rides high in the water bristling with spiky fur and the suggestion of gossamer wings.

While it is not my One Fly choice, I have to confess sheepishly to favoring one fly of this description, the White Wulff. When the sun starts to disappear in the early evening, I try to tell myself I saw a hatch of tiny white fluffy things, and I'm matching the hatch. But the truth is that it's white. I can see it clearly in the twilight, and, dammit, I'm here to see the take.

So the one-fly choice has to be something else. I'm going with the all-purpose fly, an Adams, or its cousin, the Elk Hair Caddis. If you press me between the two, give me the Elk Hair. When it skitters over the stream on the retrieve, it's catnip to the brookies. You can sometimes map the location of a dozen trout within the radius of your cast with just a few skittering retrieves. Then, set the Elk Hair drifting over where you saw the splashes, and the little guys come out to play. And even if it's drowned and bedraggled, you can retrieve it slowly as a streamer just beneath the surface.

But wait, there's more! It's also hardy; it holds up cast after cast without coming apart. And it just plain works: I have carefully unhooked this fly from the jaw of more trout than any other.

———

The sage voice of Guy weighs in:

It is pretty easy for me to narrow my choice of One Fly down to three finalists: a Wood Special, a Hornberg, or an Elk Hair Caddis.

The Wood Special is my all-time favorite fly. As a standard-size streamer, it reliably hooks larger fish. Larger meaning above average for whatever water you are fishing. A smaller version, known to The Boys as Dave's Woody (of course Dave's Woody would be smaller!), is better for the shallower water in the Grant. In either size, a Wood Special has a serious drawback in the One Fly decision: it's a streamer. You fish it beneath the surface where you may not get to see the action—which is the fun part of these endeavors.

Fishing with a streamer is like making love to a gorgeous woman with your eyes closed. Surely you will enjoy all the passion and sensual satisfaction, but wouldn't you rather watch the excitement unfold? The Wood Special will take larger fish, but I wouldn't want to have to fish a streamer all weekend long and forego the opportunity to catch fish on the surface with a dry fly. So the Wood Special is out. Down goes Dave's Woody.

I am confident many of The Boys will name the Hornberg as a top choice. We catch a ton of fish on Hornbergs, both on the surface as a dry fly (imitating a caddis fly) and below the surface retrieved wet (as a minnow). This wet/dry versatility is key if you only get one fly. (As a side note, all of us have caught fish while inadvertently dragging a Hornberg in the water while wading. This can be made less humiliating by doing it "on purpose.") The Hornberg, however, has one major drawback: poor durability. I recall someone (Phil, Klingon, others?) catching a bunch of fish on the same individual Hornberg over several days, but that is rare. More commonly, they fall apart after catching a few fish, losing a wing or the hackle. So because of durability concerns for the one-fly criterion, I would pass on the Hornberg.

Which leaves the Elk Hair Caddis as my top choice. Like a Hornberg, an Elk Hair Caddis can be floated as a dry, and then retrieved wet, like a Muddler Minnow. I am not exaggerating by saying I have caught hundreds of fish at the Grant on an Elk Hair Caddis. One morning on the upper Dead, I caught more than twenty-five small brookies on an Elk Hair in a couple hours.

To make it even better, I would use an orange-body version, which is similar to a Dave's Woody except that it will float as a dry fly. I would tie it myself with a #12 hook and the body made of orange sparkle dubbing material. In fly-tying jargon, it is made of grizzly rooster saddle hackle, palmered down the body for legs, with standard brownish-black elk hair for the down wing and head, plus strong black thread with extra glue to keep it durable. There it is, ready to rumble, fished dry on the surface, dancing shallow in the current, or deep on sinking line. Boom.

————

Billy's modest thoughts:

Here's the truth of the matter: I'm a saltwater guy by heritage and, after eighteen years or so of fishing the Grant once a year, I'm only just beginning to approach competence when it comes to trout. My quarry growing up were croakers, speckled sea trout, redfish, Spanish mackerel, bluefish, striped bass, bonito, and, later, tuna. With little thought I can throw a plug 100 yards with spinning gear and put it within a foot or so of where I want it. If you talk to me about Cast Masters, Sluggos, Broken-Back Rebels, or the Aubergine Yo-Zuri Deep Diver, I'm all over it.

Not so much when it comes to trout and trout flies. On the Swift and Dead Diamond rivers I am a neophyte and occasionally a poser. I can cast reasonably well (indeed I love to practice getting that perfect loop for laying a fly down quietly), but getting an unimpeded dead drift is a skill that I can muster only occasionally. In the Foreword to this book, Lou Zambello refers to The Boys of the Grant as a wolf pack, rather than a bunch of hyenas (which seems rather generous of him). If the metaphor is accurate, I am the pup with large paws into which he has not yet grown.

It's no surprise then that I'm kind of vague on fly names. I know only a few. Here they are: Hornberg, Elk Hair Caddis, Muddler, Woolly Bugger, Wood Special (this mostly because Guy ties them and my admiration is retained in memory), and finally the category nymphs and bead head nymphs. I have lots of other flies in my case, but I'll be darned if I know what they're called. If you say Quill Gordon or Green Drake to me, I will look at you blankly, although I suspect I own a few.

The important thing to realize is that my fly memory is influenced by success. The flies I remember are those I've caught fish on despite my general lack of expertise (other than nymphs, but they're so recognizable they don't count). And so I submit that my favorite-fly nomination should carry extra evidentiary weight of the "If he can do it . . ." variety.

Hands down, my favorite fly is the Hornberg, named (I have just discovered, after a quick Google search) for Frank Hornberg, a Wisconsin game warden who originated it in the 1920s. It's practically a cliché that you can fish the Hornberg dry or wet, and my general approach is to do both: casting upstream, attempting a satisfactory dead drift, and then retrieving the fly cross current as a streamer in a series of sharp retrieves.

I've actually caught a lot of fish that way. Mostly, they are seven to ten inchers of the "I'll bite anything" category, but there was one time when I managed a short chapter of glorious success. We were fishing at the Bridge near Gate Camp, the water was high and moving fast. As I stood on the bank thinking about my strategy I saw a large white flash behind one of the rocks in the middle of the stream. I cast my trusty Hornberg upstream and for once it drifted exactly as I wanted. As it passed the rock, my fish (it already belonged to me) struck hard but missed. I put another drift in the same spot and—*bam!*—the fish took the Hornberg hard and was off and running before I could even think to set the hook.

It was then that I realized I was dealing with a monster. For the next ten minutes, I desperately matched wits with the fish, convinced that my tippet would break any second, and I would lose him. But eventually he tired, and I worked him into the shallows. He (or she— who can tell?) was more than fifteen inches long and very fat. Not the biggest trout I've seen at the Grant but right up there. With shaking hands I extracted the hook. As the fish swam back into the stream, it hit me that a net would not be a ridiculously optimistic purchase, and that the Hornberg is surely the king of the Swift and Dead Diamond rivers.

————

Ed, too, likes the Hornberg, even when using his funky tenkara equipment:

I usually succumb to local tradition and search for the brook trout with various colors of the Hornberg fly. When we stop at the local fly shop, LL Cote, I can't keep myself from picking up a variety of Hornberg colors and sizes. But I struggle with the options. Will the brown one be more effective than the yellow? What about bigger flies with the water so high? As they say, flies catch more fishermen than fish, and I find myself being hooked by the thought of missing out on one of the hot patterns during that year.

————

This is Phil back again, and now that you've heard from each of The Boys, I'm happy to share my own thoughts on the One Fly question I posed at the beginning of this chapter.

So, several of my colleagues voted for the Elk Hair Caddis and Hornberg, and Bob likes the Muddler. All good choices, and I'll even say that Bob's pick might be the most productive, though the least fun. The Hornberg seems to win by a nose.

I'm a total Hornberg bigot, but I'll surprise The Boys by saying that there is a caveat. If "one fly" literally means a single physical fly, there's a problem with the Hornberg. As Guy suggested, with use, the feathers on a Hornberg wear and tend to do it in such a way as to warp and turn the fly into a propeller. If you're using an aging Hornberg as a streamer, after a bit it will twist up your leader like crazy.

For all the reasons stated, the Hornberg is most versatile, the best all-around pattern. If you have a handful, you are good. However, if you needed to survive on a single fly, a very well tied Elk Hair or Muddler might better serve.

It's an interesting thought experiment, though the real answer is that you don't want just one fly. You want at least a little variety. With the exception of Dave "Can I Borrow a Fly?" Klinges, we all have a much larger assortment than we really need for June in the Grant. I think we are all in close agreement that a fine Grant Selection comprising a goodly mix of Hornbergs, Elk Hairs, Muddlers, Woolly Buggers, Wood Specials, and even Dave's tiny little Woody would serve one very well. Add in some Adamses and other mayfly imita-tors— perhaps a Goddard Caddis, some Humpies, and a nymph or two—and you are more than good to go. For each pattern, you want at least a couple of different sizes (10s, 12s, and 14s are about right for the Grant) and a good rule of thumb is three of each size, so we are still talking more than sixty flies.

By the way, the guys at LL Cote seem pretty knowledgeable about flies, but they are generally not very tuned in to what goes on in the

Grant. They just don't get the opportunity to fish there. Although not so many miles away, the waters most of their patrons fish are bigger, slower, and usually stocked. Pretty different from the unusual native trout streams in the Grant. So our little colloquy about the One Fly just may be the best local knowledge you will find.

A Case for Un-waders

By Phil Odence

John Gierach titled a book *Death, Taxes, and Leaky Waders*. In those five words, Gierach captures the love-hate relationship all fishermen have with the bulkiest fishing equipment they own. Waders. Can't live with 'em, can't live without 'em. Well, I pretty much decided I could live without them, at least for mid-June trips to the Grant.

There's nothing more annoying than the feeling of a wet, icy intrusion into the dry sanctity of one's socks. Usually, you first sense it much higher, at the side of your knee, the back of your thigh, or the top of the boot. But water being water, and gravity and fishing being so persistent, inevitably what starts as a dribble turns into a damp sock and then a soaked sock, and soon you find yourself cursing the *squawunch* of a puddled boot with every step. The only silver lining is the amusement afforded your compadres, delayed due to your stoic silence about your unfortunate condition until you strip down and, to their great delight, water the stream-side flora with ounce upon amusing ounce from your waders turned watering can.

It's almost always on just one side, the asymmetry making discomfort all the worse, a dry foot serving as a constant reminder of how it is supposed to be in a perfect fishing world, thus subverting any possibility of persuading yourself that one wet foot is not so bad. It *is* so bad. It sucks. Oh, the humanity. Fucking waders.

So, I stopped wearing them.

What I stopped wearing was and still is a pair of twenty-five-year-old cheap Red Balls with integrated felt bottom boots. They are that shade of brown that otherwise can only be found in Carhartt work pants. Their tubby cut always brings to mind stories of unlucky anglers taking a tumble or a wave "over the gunnels" and being carried downstream or out to sea, sometimes fatally. But, luckily, Red Balls sport a braided shoestring to cinch the top and obviate any such danger. What's more, when navigating dense stream-side brush, the Red Ball's tough canvas exterior shrugs off the nastiest thorns and is scarcely marred by the coarsest bark or granite crag.

My biggest problem over the years has had nothing to do with water, but rather the chaffing from the abrupt top edge of the stiff rubber boot. Not so much an issue in the water, but a long hike from the car to a remote spot has often left me suffering raw pink welts just below my calves.

My less tolerant, less parsimonious (read: more sensible?) mates have long since upgraded to stocking-foot waders with comfort-able-looking boots. That design seems to take care of the chaffing problem. But whether they are the nylon, rubber, neoprene, or fancy breathable sort of waders, leaking is, well, like death and taxes.

The old Red Balls have held up better than fancier brands and styles, but eventually, they too succumbed to leakage as the rubber lost some of its youthful flexibility. I imagine that if I'd been better about hanging them up in the basement after each use, I might have gotten a few more years out of them. I will say they've scared the shit out of me a few times, suspended in the dark bowels of my home and looking like the victim of a lynching, which may explain my weakness for not storing them properly. Anyway, eventually tiny holes began to appear here and there. The patch tape that came with the waders served me quite well in a decade-long battle, but as the campaign waged on, skir-mishes became more frequent.

———

Mid-June weather in the Grant is variable. We've huddled by the wood stove on persistently chilly and rainy weekends and have sweltered through nights naked and sweaty atop our sleeping bags. It was on a trip at the hotter end of the scale that I finally said, "Screw it!" and lost the Red Balls.

Thankfully, for fishing's sake, the June waters of the Swift and the Dead are pretty cool generally, even in sunny weather, and partic-ularly in the morning. Thus, sans waders, the first step into the chilly water is usually enough to trigger a sharp gasp. But, as the body adjusts and as the day warms, shock turns to tolerable and then to pleasant. On a hot day, it is now hard for me to imagine any other way to fish.

An un-wader rig is pretty simple. My inaugural outfit comprised old Brooks Brothers cotton khakis and a pair of particularly porous red, white, and blue Saucony running shoes. You want shoes that drain water easily for a quick recovery when you step up onto a rock or the bank. A nice side benefit of the un-wader: since starting the practice, I'm usually the first guy out on the water and the first guy ready to load up to head back for lunch.

My experiments were not without a learning curve, and I've evolved my un-wader getup a bit over the years. The first problem I had to contend with is one that anyone with stocking-foot waders has also run into: sand and grit in the shoes. It's a mostly tolerable annoyance, although sometimes a sharp pebble can necessitate a sit-down on a rock or the bank. Tying shoes tightly alleviates the problem, but not entirely, and you can't find gaiters that work with running shoes.

Problem two: the riverbeds in the Grant are fairly chunky in places, and your foot often finds the gap between boulders. In boots you don't notice the way your foot and ankle occasionally jam against rocks, but with sneakers you can find yourself a bit bruised up after a day of wading. Traction can be an issue that exacerbates this problem. The waffle bottoms of my Sauconys were good under some wading conditions, but they fared poorly on slimy rocks, contributing to the ankle banging.

I formulated a grand plan involving Shoe Goo and felt pads, but had a hard time finding the thick felt I needed. You're probably way ahead of me here, and, yes, I eventually concluded that wading boots were the answer. A couple of wrinkles: my aforementioned tight-fisted nature and the issue of socks. To combat the sand and gravel problem, I had tried wool socks with the sneakers. It certainly diminished the gravel problem, but sopping socks turned out to be heavy, droopy, and annoying.

And, I was not certain that conventional wading boots would fit and operate without socks. Searching the web, I stumbled across a pair of fourteen-dollar retro canvas wading boots. Imagine a pair of vintage Chuck Taylors, the color of a faded Olive Muddler, with big fat felt pads on bottom. In short, the perfect un-wader shoe.

They are not perfect, but they're pretty good. They lace up tight just above the ankle. Some junk sneaks in, but not much. (Perhaps one day I'll experiment with some borrowed gaiters, but I like to keep it simple.) And they only chafe a little. The felt bottoms provide as good traction as any. I have a feeling I may never have to replace these boots.

———

I'm in pretty good shape with pants as well. Khakis are fine, but if you wear them cuffed, you'll find yourself pausing occasionally to dump collected sand. I experimented with shorts and that's not a bad route under some conditions. But if the bugs are in a mood or you find yourself bushwhacking, you want to have the legs covered. The other problem with good cotton khakis is that they stay wet and heavy. Not a deal-breaker, but the weight of sopping, slow-drying cotton will have me hoisting them up regularly to avoid the plumber's-smile look. Perhaps braces would mitigate the issue. There's also the practical problem of a wet seat when I get back in my car, but I avoid that issue by riding in someone else's car.

Eventually, I popped twenty-two dollars at LL Cote for a pair of poly-nylon, khaki-colored pants with no cuffs. The legs zip off at the knees, so I can convert them into shorts. Overall, a really good solution. Even soaked, they aren't particularly heavy and they dry rapidly. For a complete quick dry, it works well to go commando or, maybe, with nylon or poly undies.

So that's it. Canvas wading boots and light nylon trousers, and I'm perfectly good to go for late spring conditions.

You'd think I might have had some success in influencing the other Boys of the Grant, but not so much. Bob has given it a go a few times; the rest of The Boys are wed to conventional outfitting. I'm accustomed to being an outlier from my habit of barefoot running, which is not dissimilar in terms of being unconventional, back to basics, and non-intuitive. It's been five years since I've run in shoes and nary an acquaintance has followed the lone trail I've blazed. In my shod days, I was bugged by winter slush through the top of my shoes. It's ironic that I now brave winter weather in bare feet. Nor is the irony lost on me that I have discarded the waders to avoid wet feet. But, hey, it works for me.

Do I miss waders? Ever? As best I can, I keep my old pair patched for cold conditions, but I've not pulled them on in several Junes. I just don't need 'em. There is that one particular moment, though: You're in up to mid-thigh and step into a hole, thus allowing a sharp, icy assault on—how do I say it delicately? Any guy who's swum in a mountain lake or off the coast of Maine understands the issue. No matter how temperate the air, the instant the water reaches scrotum level, all I can think about is my Red Balls.

Privy to Privies

By David Van Wie

There is an old saying that the outhouse is fifty feet too close in the summer and fifty feet too far in the winter. Few people in America today have firsthand experience with this phenomenon. After many years visiting the Grant, The Boys can confirm that the old saying is undeniably true.

Every cabin in the Grant has an outhouse, or privy. Visiting the outhouse, with its assault on the nostrils, is an essential part of the remote experience. By essential, I mean, well, essential. Unless you use the outhouse, your only alternative for doing what bears do in the woods would be to do it in the woods. With the bears.

We Boys proudly tolerate the unpleasantness of the outhouse stench with a sort of chip on our collective shoulder. Our fortitude and forbearance come with good humor, and perhaps a bit of superiority. Over the years, we have seen visitors squirm with the experience, gag even, and then choose not to return due to the primitive facilities. This winnowing out of marginal visitors is, to us, a good thing.

While outhouses may be distant cousins to portapotties, they have much more charm. Okay, maybe not charm. More something, though: Tradition? Torment? Time travel? In truth, outhouses may not have much charm, but they do have bugs. Spiders, mosquitoes, sow bugs, centipedes, and other crawly things contribute to that winnowing effect I was just talking about.

There are various tactics for coping with the smell. My wife brings her own can of air freshener to spray as she *goes in*. You don't need to spray it on the way out, because you shouldn't feel embarrassed about leaving an unpleasant odor for the next person. There is nothing you did in there alone to make it smell that bad, so why worry?

Some of The Boys bring a cigar into the outhouse. This both

covers the smell and keeps the bugs away. But, replacing one stench with another doesn't suit everyone, as some of us are of the opinion that the oral regret over the next few days outweighs any immediate satisfaction or bug-repelling benefit that may come from smoking a cigar.

A traditional method to control the outhouse aroma is to dump ashes from the wood stove into the pit as daily cover for the doo-doo. This method is only marginally effective and isn't always an available option in the warmer seasons, when the wood stove is rarely in use. In winter, the freezing temperatures keep the fragrance at bay, so spring and fall are the only times when ashes do the trick.

As much as I love Hellgate Gorge Cabin, with its spectacular view of the upper gorge, the cabin builders made a serious meteorological and olfactory blunder by putting the outhouse about fifty feet southwest of the cabin, thus allowing the prevailing breeze to waft the odor toward the cabin, making it truly "fifty feet too close in the summer." I really notice it when I sit on the cabin steps to put on my boots. Fortunately, the screens on the porch manage to foil not only the bugs, but also, as illogical as it may sound, most of the malodorous zephyrs that carry the ripe smell toward the cabin.

The outhouse at Sam's Cabin is far enough away through the trees, behind the woodshed. Apparently, the woodshed-between-the-privy-and-cabin strategy is a proven one that has a long tradition. Too bad cabin builders didn't use it more often in the Grant.

When my wife was visiting Stoddard Cabin on her mountain bike one summer, she observed immediately that the outhouse there is *way* too far from the cabin, not only for winter but also in the summer. I mentioned the mosquitoes, didn't I?

The privy at the Management Center is very close to the cabin, but downwind. Thankfully, the Management Center has an indoor flush toilet in summer, so the privy gets little use after the last freeze, thus limiting, if not eliminating, the outhouse smell in warm weather. Yet seven guys in a cabin with one indoor toilet has its own charm, especially after last night's beer and chili rendezvous with that second cup of coffee after breakfast.

———

No, it didn't snow in June. This shot of the Management Center outhouse is from a frosty February trip.

After many years of visiting the Grant once a year in June, I started to ask myself why I didn't get up there more often. So several years ago, my wife, Cheryl, and I started going a couple of times each winter with friends from the Portland area. Winter at the Grant is spectacular, with great Nordic skiing and snowshoeing. The cabin is cozy with the wood stove blazing, and the privies only add to the adventure. In winter, of course, the stink is not the problem. Nor are the bugs. Rather, it is the "fifty feet too far" problem. And, of course, when you do complete the fifty-foot sojourn you are rewarded with a cold seat. A *really* cold seat.

　　It is 2:00 a.m. on a Saturday in February. The Sandman has left everyone in the cabin in deep slumber, but now in his place, Tinklebell is awakening Cheryl from Dreamland. The cabin has cooled down considerably as the fire in the wood stove has died back to a bed of coals. A toasty warm sleeping bag hugs her in the chill air. But Tinklebell is pressing on her bladder, like a cat preparing a place to lie down. "Time to get up!" says Tinklebell. The Sandman isn't coming back until Tinklebell is sent packing.

Unzzzzzzzzzip goes the bag, as quietly as possible, with Cheryl trying not to wake the others. She sits up and touches her feet to the cold floor, her toes searching for her slippers, placed strategically for just this occasion. Finding them, she grabs a headlamp from the frosty windowsill and reaches for her winter parka on the bedpost. Her hat and mittens are in the sleeve. Shielding the light to provide just enough illumination to make it across the main room without waking anyone, Cheryl pads toward the back door and slides her feet from her slippers and into her winter boots, also placed in anticipation of an early morning trip to the outhouse.

Despite her effort, the door latch clatters as she steps out from the relative warmth of the cabin into the piercing dry cold of the February night. Her breath puffs a cloud into the moonlight. The thermometer on the porch reads minus 15°F. Naturally, the seat in the privy will be the same temperature. But now the outhouse seems to be about seven miles from the porch. Gamely, Cheryl steps off into the crunching snow and trudges down the shoveled path, with waist-high snow banks on either side.

After a frigid encounter with the seat, she reverses the trek, makes it back inside, and snuggles into her bag, which in her brief absence has conveniently cooled nearly to cabin temperature. Tinklebell vanquished, soon Cheryl is warm and toasty again, waiting for the Sandman to return.

This Siberian trek to the outhouse is what separates the truly committed—my dear wife is the consummate adventurer—from the curious one-time visitor.

Instead of visiting the frosty privy at night, men have the option of finding a place to make yellow snow much closer to the cabin without freezing their tushes off. Cabin etiquette calls for the men to at least go around the corner somewhere so the yellow snow is hidden from view.

Such etiquette only applies in mixed company, I have observed.

One winter I stopped by Sam's Cabin when it was inhabited by a bunch of recently graduated young men who, thanks to considerable beer consumption, had created an impressive yellow stalagmite a few feet outside their back door.

For both men and women, there are techniques to mitigate the cold-seat problem when visiting the privy. Covering the seat with strips of toilet paper, approximating the oval shape, is the standard method of providing a small amount of insulation for your bottom. One year we found a seat cover made from plastic foam packaging wrap cut to shape. Obviously this was made by someone at home, and must have involved way too much apprehension, not to mention fastidious planning.

More consistent with the rustic hunting cabin motif, there is a deerskin-covered toilet seat, with deer hair intact, hanging on the wall in Merrill Brook Cabin. It sure looks warm and comfy, but it is probably more for show than practical use.

———

Sitting in the outhouse in summer or winter, one has time to ponder important cosmic questions, like, "Why there is a moon in the outhouse door?" It seems that most of the privies in the Grant have them.

This is a much-debated question. One story is that rural school outhouses had a sun or star for the boys' side and a moon for the girls' side, or both on a unisex privy. Cartoonists, notably Al Capp in his Li'l Abner strip, made the quarter moon a symbol to help identify the outhouse, and it has stuck in popular culture and still adorns many.

The practical purpose for a cutout in the door is to provide ventilation and light. Some privies also have a small-screened window on the side as a welcome option to let in some fresh air at nose level. In winter, one can close the little shutter on the window to keep out the cold north wind or blowing snow.

———

One night we Boys were sleeping in Hellgate Hilton when just after midnight we heard a tremendous rasping sound outside. It was an indescribable noise that echoed across the valley. Pretty scary, actually. After fifteen minutes of this bizarre racket, two of us finally got up the nerve to investigate, creeping out into the dark night with a flashlight and tiptoeing through the pine needles more in trepidation than to be quiet.

The sound was clearly coming from the privy. "What could be making that noise *in the outhouse?*" Bob mumbled. Everyone in our party was present and accounted for in their bunks. Maybe Bigfoot was in there after eating the leftover chili we had dumped out back.

As we approached, the sound grew louder. Our flashlight beam cut into the darkness, but only a few yards ahead. Slowly we advanced, until we saw it: a stout porcupine, gnawing on the plywood wall of the outhouse. With millions of trees all around us, the porcupine was eating the outhouse? Really?

The sound amplification was similar to how a grand piano broadcasts the vibrations of its strings into a concert hall: the plywood and the outhouse structure intensified the sound to create a dreadful nighttime cacophony that had struck fear into our weary souls.

We chased the porky away, and everyone was happy to get back to sleep. I learned later that porcupines like the salt in the glue used to fabricate plywood, so this critter was scraping away on the wall with his teeth to get to the glue. Oh, the wonders of the wild!

The Fallen Soldier

By David Klinges

I t was the end of another beautiful June day of fishing, one where you don't want to leave the stream unless your last cast lands a trout. Three of us were in the car headed back to Gate Camp— Billy, Norm, and me. As we came around a turn heading east towards the entrance to the Grant, a car approached traveling in the opposite direction. We slowed to greet some fellow fishermen, and immediately recognized former Dean of the College Ralph Manuel. By this time, Ralph had retired, but he'd been dean of the College when we were undergraduates and so would always be "our dean."

We slowed to wave and pay our regards and thought it somewhat odd that the other car came to a full stop. The look of concern on the faces of Ralph and the car's other occupant, David Bradley, immediately brought us up short.

They were searching for their buddy Fred, and wondered had we seen anyone? The story was not good. They had separated from their friend at lunch, and it was now approaching 8:00 p.m. He had a form of Parkinson's and was not fit to be wandering in the woods. They had gotten in touch with New Hampshire Fish and Game, but the authorities wouldn't be able to get anyone to Wentworth's Location to conduct a search before June's late nightfall, and it would be dark in little more than an hour.

Ralph and David gratefully accepted our offer to help them, so we headed upstream to the vicinity of where they thought their friend had been fishing. Our strategy was to walk parallel courses to the stream keeping a lookout for their missing comrade or any evidence that he had been in the area. To those not familiar with the Great North Woods of New Hampshire, this effort would prove daunting. Hundreds of years of foliage growth, dead and rotting in the proximity of the Dead

Diamond, have created a bog that is littered with fallen trees. Some of these downed trees are monumental. Simply moving fifty yards in a straight line would be a challenge even for men younger than us.

The task was terrifying and exhilarating at the same time. This was literally life or death. Leaving a man in his seventies in the woods at night was not an option, and he had already been on his own for over eight hours without his medication. As we searched, it became apparent that there were distinct footprints that jumped out at us from the muck. But they were moose prints. I had never considered how clear a print a 1,200-pound animal could make as he forages in the woods.

As the search continued, our initial eagerness to find the lost fly fisherman—we had felt certain we would find him—melted into despair. We could uncover no evidence of human disturbance anywhere we looked, and the enormity of the task began to weigh on us. The implications of the fading sunlight were as apparent to us and the other desperate searchers as a classroom clock ticking towards 3:00 p.m. is to a seventh grader.

Eventually, it became clear that simply getting back to the road would be a challenge in the deepening dusk, and we reluctantly turned back in the direction of the cars. Shortly thereafter we were further sobered to learn that a third group had been searching the river near Monahan's Bathtub, where Fred had last been seen. They hadn't found a trace of him either, but even the idea of their looking in the water expanded our fears about what could have befallen the poor guy.

That night in the cabin, The Boys did not engage in our typically uproarious dinner banter. The tone was somber and we spoke quietly about what was going on. Even our less eventful trips to the Grant engender self-reflection, just by the nature of the surroundings and the wilderness experience itself. No sound but the wind, water, birds, and bugs; little evidence of the human condition. Our conversation that night wandered around all sorts of what-ifs. What if the searchers were unsuccessful in finding Fred or what if he was not found alive? If it had to be this way, having one's life come to an end in this special place seemed like an acceptable fate (at the right time, of course) to those of us gathered in the Gate Camp that evening.

Sitting on the porch after dinner, we weren't surprised to see Dean Ralph and Dave Bradley drive up later in the night. Gate Camp has the

only phone in the Grant (we were miles from cell coverage). They had
come to make a call to Fred's wife and report his disappearance. The
mood on the porch darkened.

While no one wanted to say aloud what everyone was thinking,
over the next hour we held what could only be described as a wake.
Our guests were offered several fingers of Tennessee's finest sour mash
whiskey, and the lost friend was remembered with tales of many years
of trips to the Grant. The older group of alums had been making their
annual trip to the Grant for twice the number of years we had. Some
of their stories made us laugh—the Dean was always as a great racon-
teur—but it did not escape us how naturally they had slipped into the
past tense in referencing their old friend. At one point, Ralph ended
a thought about Fred with "God rest his soul," nervously adding, "if
need be."

The shared experiences bound us tightly together that night. We
felt privileged to be spending time with Ralph and Dave, mourning
together what we feared to be the loss of a kindred spirit.

The night will go on record as the most active ever in the Grant.
A seemingly never-ending procession of northbound vehicles, some
loaded with dogs, disturbed the quietude of the wood. Search-and-
rescue copters cut through the darkness with bright spotlights.

Late into the night, we sprung awake to a knock on the door of
the cabin and the sound of voices on the porch. Any kind of disturbance in the Grant is disquieting given the peacefulness of the woods,
and this one did not bode well. With surprise and delight, we saw
a uniformed Fish and Game warden alongside Ralph and Dave and
they were smiling. They needed to use the phone again, this time to
inform Fred's wife that our Fallen Soldier had been found in the early
morning hours by Fish and Game search dogs. And, remarkably, he was
in reasonably good condition.

Thanks to the tracking hounds, he was discovered even though
he was nowhere near the stream where he was thought to be fishing.
He had headed in the wrong direction following his lunch break with
Ralph and Dave. What had been an incredibly harrowing experience for
us was even more extraordinary for its happy ending.

In following years, we were pleased to see Ralph's full comple-
ment of friends at the Grant, including the once-missing comrade. Each

encounter brings a hint of our own mortality, but also a reminder that we all look forward to many more years of our annual outing.

———

After I wrote my account of The Fallen Soldier story, Guy found the logbook entry from that weekend in Sam's Cabin. We had never read this entry before. Here is the same story from a different perspective, as written by Dave Bradley '58.

Sam's Cabin Log Entry:
June 12 – 15, 2008- Thursday to Sunday

This year will be remembered as the most dramatic of the 37 years of the Old Dean's Annual Grant Trips.

Longtime member Fred Appleton, Hobart Class of '57, went missing when he failed to show up at an agreed upon rendezvous at 12:30 pm with the Old Dean, Ralph Manuel '58 on Friday. Fred who has Parkinson's disease had as always insisted on fishing alone and was dropped off by Ralph at the road to Monahan's Bathtub a little before 10 am. When Fred failed to show, Ralph began a search for him, eventually driving over 50 miles back and forth on Dead Diamond Road. Ralph sought the help of Dave Bradley '58 and Dick Pew '58 who were canoeing the Upper Dead by leaving them a note on the car Dave and Dick had stashed at Slewgundy. Dave and Dick got off the water about a half hour later and joined the search for Fred.

Dick and Dave enlisted 3 canoeists to sweep the river upstream from Monahan's, and Dick and Dave swept the river from Monahan's down for about 500 yards.

When no sign of Fred showed up, Ralph went to the Grant caretaker, Lorraine Turner, who called "search and rescue" about 5:30 pm. Over the next 8+ hours the Grant was invaded by about 5 Fish and Game officials (who enlisted a cadre of volunteers from other cabins), 2 State Troopers in their cruiser, a State Police helicopter, and 6 or 7 carloads of volunteer professional searchers with trained dogs.

Jim Strickler '50 (also an old dean of the Medical School) arrived a day late just as the search was getting started in earnest. Shortly after dusk, Dave and Ralph decided to call their wives who are close friends with Fred's wife, Pat, to be on standby to go to Pat's house if the news of Fred's situation turned out badly.

By about 11 pm, the group made the decision that we had to

call Pat even though we knew she could do nothing from Hanover to help. So another trip to the Gate Camp and the nearest phone. As Ralph and I drove there, Ralph started to beat up on himself for letting Fred fish alone and by then we were both thinking Fred would not be found alive. The phone conversation with Pat (both of us talked with her) was about as tough an assignment as either of us ever experienced.

None of the 5 of us were asked to be volunteers ("we don't need another old man lost in the woods") so we went to bed. I, at least, managed to fall asleep. At just after 2 am Lorraine came to my bedroom window and said "The dogs found him, and he is alright. He was in the woods just above the Bathtub."

It turned out that Fred after being dropped off had tried to walk into the holes above Monahan's where the old dump was. He got into dense underbrush, fell on his back in what he described as a "mud pot" and could not get up. He never got to the river and spent 15+ hours in that situation before he was found at about 1:30 am.

Fred had heard people calling him, but his voice was too weak to make his replies heard until one of the K-9 volunteer searchers and his dog "Able" heard him. The volunteer had come all the way from Burlington, VT.

We were told that the dogs are trained to smell any human being in the woods, but it seemed the searcher first heard Fred before the dog smelled him. The searcher zeroed in on the location by asking Fred to respond by saying "Able." About 20' from Fred the dog indicated he had the location by jumping into his handler's arms.

The third trip to the Gate camp to make the call to Pat was marked by 2 emotions: joy and anger with a touch of humor. "That stupid son-a-bitch, he got out of cooking the ham."

Everything else about our stay was so anti-climactic that it is hard to write about. But I did catch a 13-1/2" brookie in the lower Dead late on Saturday."

—Dave Bradley

————

We were saddened to learn of Fred Appleton's passing in August 2013. Though we didn't know him well—only from friendly hellos stream side—we learned that he was a remarkable and well-loved physician and professor at Dartmouth Medical School. According to his obituary in

The Diamond Peaks tower over Dave Klinges making his way to the Swift Diamond River.

Guy landed this colorful brook trout caught while canoeing on the upper Dead Diamond River. Photo by Jill Osgood.

The Boys have toasted the end of many enjoyable days while watching the sun set over the Swift Diamond from Sam's Lookout.

Bob and Ed are outfitted and ready for battle.

A trout divulges its location with concentric rings while rising to small flies at Sid Hayward Ledge.

Bob gets lucky in The Pool of No Luck.

The rushing waters through Hellgate Gorge have scoured the ledge rocks smooth over the eons. Pete Blodgett Cabin is nestled in the meadow across the swimming hole.

The run and pool above the entrance to Hellgate Gorge offer some great fishing plus an awe-inspiring view of Finnson's Cliff.

Hag Trout. Watercolor by Robert Chamberlin, 2015.

DVW and Guitar. Watercolor by Robert Chamberlin, 2006.

Dave K Casting. Watercolor by Robert Chamberlin, 2013.

Phil Hooks Up. Watercolor by Robert Chamberlin, 2013.

Rising Trout (after James Prosek). Watercolor by Robert Chamberlin, 2013.

Bogie. Watercolor by Robert Chamberlin, 2013.

Still Life With Yukon Jack.
Watercolor by Robert
Chamberlin, 2014.

Changing Flies. Watercolor by
Robert Chamberlin, 2013.

Norm on Doug's Rock. Watercolor by Robert Chamberlin, 2013.

Jack's World. Watercolor by Robert Chamberlin, 2015.

Hellgate Hilton. Watercolor & Ink by Phil Odence, 2002.

Outhouse Afternoon. Watercolor & Ink by Phil Odence, 2002.

Gate Camp Bridge. Watercolor & Ink by Phil Odence, 2008.

Management Center from Sam's Cabin. Watercolor by Phil Odence, 2005.

Wood Special

Hornberg

Muddler Minnow

Adams

Woolly Bugger

Elk Hair Caddis

Flies tied by David Van Wie.

Billy drifts a dry fly in the pool near Doug's Rock. Photo by Robert Chamberlin.

Phil, Norm and Guy enjoyed early fall colors at Sid Hayward Ledge during the Make-up Trip.

Bob blends in, mostly, with the green vegetation near Monahan's Bathtub.

Guy's brother, Doug, a regular in the early years, captured this amazing shot of a brook trout he caught on an Elk Hair Caddis in the clear water of the Swift Diamond.

Slewgundy at sundown, but no signs of another epic hatch like the one Phil experienced on his first night in the Grant.

High water roars down through Little Garfield Falls.

The Valley News, Dr. Appleton was twice named Outstanding Teacher of the Year by his students and peers. He was an avid runner and sports fan, a fixture at Dartmouth athletic events and his grandchildren's games. He loved fly-fishing, and was a regular member of the Old Dean's group that has been going to the Grant for more than forty years. Just before his death, Fred celebrated fifty-five years of marriage with his wife, Pat. He is missed by his family, his colleagues, and his fishing buddies. We hope the trout are always rising in heaven.

The One Fish

By Phil Odence

One fish taught me more in twenty minutes than I've gleaned from any how-to fly-fishing book.

Elsewhere I've called this business "the multi-dimensional, never-solved fly-fishing conundrum," and I can't improve upon that description. I know a lot more than I did twenty years ago—particularly when it comes to finding trout in the Grant—but I'm far from satisfied.

Guy catches more fish than any of us. Bob might come in second. We don't keep individual counts—okay, we do, but we don't obsess over them. Clearly, though, Guy catches more. And Guy has fished more, much more, and he's fished with very good fishermen like Lou Zambello. What it comes down to is that he has a keen understanding of trout behavior, of what makes them tick.

Guy will tell you that trout are very good at one thing: getting as much to eat as they can while expending a minimum amount of energy. Trout are purpose built (by the invisible hands of natural selection). It's all they do, so they get very good at it. There's my problem. I do things other than fish. If I were a little more focused, like a trout—well, who knows?

The Orvis books (or L.L. Bean's, or whomever's) feature a line-drawn illustration of the anatomy of a stream. The visual does its best to help you understand what's under a stream's surface and where you might find yourself a fish.

Much of it comes down to the energy-minimization/food-maximization thing. The perfect hangout for a trout is a place where he can lurk effortlessly, but which, at the same time, offers a passing stream of food. That typically means slow water on the edge of faster water. What better spot than behind a rock? Like stepping around the corner of a building to avoid the wind, a trout in the flow shadow of a rock can hold position while fast water passes, under the foam line, just a couple of tail flips away. With moving water comes river flotsam, parading by for the inspection of the patient trout. Some of the stuff warrants closer inspection and occasionally turns out to be something worthy of a good chomp.

It's simple in concept, but I never feel like I really know where the fish are—until I see some evidence, of course. A few of the other guys seem to be more confident. I understand the theory from the books, but, for whatever reason, I don't seem to have the ability to assemble all the visual data into a three-dimensional picture of what's under the surface.

A great example is a pool on the Swift Diamond, only a little upstream from where the road swings to the bank and just above the Confluence. Guy visits this spot once or twice a trip and routinely encounters multiple fish. Even if I get to the water first, though, I have a hell of a time finding the spot. I just don't see it the way he does, until he's there extracting trout and making it obvious.

Having a strong sense of where the fish are is critical, because if you know they are there, you know it's worth sticking around, winding up, and throwing some junk. Otherwise, hell, you might give it a cast or two and just move on, perhaps abandoning Mr. Twelve Inches to wait for the next angler.

————

The day I encountered the One Fish, he was operating in an obvious spot, squarely behind a big rock that broke the surface, right next to a foam line, right where he ought to be. More importantly, he was quick to confirm my hypothesis. I started with a Hornberg, as I almost always do, a nice dry one. Natural color. My very first cast landed gently, about two meters upstream of the rock with loose enough leader and line to allow for a perfectly natural drift. And drift it did, slower at first, until it neared the rock and sped up into the foam atop accelerating water that bent around the near side of the rock. As the Hornberg spun around the downstream edge of the rock: *Bang!* A big flash and a splash and a nudge, and I knew that I knew where a fish was.

I let the fly drift on for a few moments before hauling my line off the water. Letting the fly dry with a few false casts, I dropped it down once again, in almost the identical spot as the previous cast. Thus, the fly traced the same path, winding into the foam by the rock and—*Bang!*

again. This time I was poised to twitch the rod back and set the hook. I might have been a bit too early, but no matter, I would have the bastard on the next try, for sure.

I hauled up the line and gave it a few back and forths for drying and again let the fly alight at the upstream end of its appointed route. In suit, it followed the path along the rock, into the foam and . . . no bang. No nothing. This time I let it drift a bit longer, just in case. But, no. Rinse and repeat. After two or three more unanswered attempts, I was scratching my head.

Fish love worms and insects, also other fish and their roe, but they are not particularly into feathers, foil, hair, or metal. No, artificial flies certainly don't taste good; rather they are fashioned to look just like things that do. A practice going back thousands of years, flies were originally tied to look like aquatic insects, but the technique has been extended to imitate other foodstuffs, including terrestrial insects, and even mice and frogs for bass fishing. A classic dry fly floats on the surface and from underwater appears to be an insect that has landed upon or is rising from the surface of the stream. Size, color, and shape are all part of the trout's recognition calculus. Get it right, "match the hatch," as they say, and you fool the fish.

The One Fish probably thought my Hornberg was a light-colored caddis fly, naturally spinning down the river in the foam. And so he gave it a poke. Maybe he missed. Maybe I pulled it out of his mouth. Maybe he aborted at the last moment because it just didn't seem right. When I cast again, thirty seconds later, he saw another coming by— same size, shape, and color—and he probably figured it was an insect from the same hatch. Maybe he was a little wary after the first time, and so approached half-heartedly. In any case, he didn't get hooked. And, after that, he changed his thinking: "Fool me three times, shame on me." Evidently, he was done with Hornbergs, at least for the time being.

Changing flies is an investment. You use up time during which you could otherwise have a line in the water. Changing too often means fishing less. Changing too infrequently means . . . you're Klingon. It's a bit of a pain. You've taken time to strip off thirty feet of line that you must first reel in. Then you need to free up your hands, attaching the rod to your vest or pinching it under an arm or between your thighs. You have to be extremely careful after you take the fly box out of your pocket and open it, lest you dump $50 worth of LL Cote's best into the stream.

Attaching a new fly to your leader is a skill unto itself. The tippet at the end is thicker than a hair, but not by much. And it's slightly stiff, though that can be used to your advantage. Poking it through the hole at the head of the fly is much like threading a needle. The knot is intricate. Oh, and I forgot to mention, you are over fifty, you can't see the tiny friggin' eyelet, and your fingers are cold and fat. It can be a bitch.

About five years ago several of us acquired (guess where) an ingenious lifesaving device: a pair of miniature, high-power magnifiers that attach to and flip down from the visor of your baseball cap. Makes you feel twenty years younger. Absent those specs, I'd be lost at fly-changing time.

You need to exercise extreme care with the knot. There is nothing worse than going through the effort of persuading a fish to hook up for dinner and having the knot give way at the moment of truth, not only losing you the fish but ipso facto a perfectly good fly along with it. I use something called a Duncan Loop. I think most of The Boys employ an Improved Clinch Knot. Either way, tying on a fly can be a project.

———

But, with the One Fish, it was obviously time for a change. I snipped off the Hornberg with the handy little clipper that hangs on a retractable holder pinned to my vest. The back end holds a sharp steel needle to poke dried glue from the hole on a new fly. My next try was an Adams, the quintessential dry fly. The Orvis catalog says it "should be in every fly box." But I picked that Adams because it *wasn't* in my fly box. It was the one dry fly stuck to the fake lambswool pad on my vest, and therefore handy. I wanted to get back to that fish quickly. With extra care, I tied on the Adams. I considered using something closer in color to the Hornberg, but would that be a good thing in this case? Anyway, I went with the Adams.

Having let the water rest a bit and after a few false casts, I dropped the Adams in precisely the same spot as my earlier casts. Towards the rock, along the near side in the foam, past the edge and—*Bang!*—there he was, and again I was unable to set the hook. I laid in another cast, just like the previous, semi-successful ones. Around the rock it went and *Ba-bing*, the same thing. Yes, he went at it a second time and with the same result. It's worth noting that while an unsuccessful consummation of a strike is frustrating, it's infinitely better than nothing at all, which is what I experienced on the next three or four casts.

The problem, I thought, might be my relatively slow reflexes. I think it's what kept me from playing college soccer, though I worked around it on the rugby pitch. While pulling in the empty line, I wondered if someone quicker might have hooked the One Fish. Shit, I'd had four tries. I pondered this as I pinched a #12 Light Cahill from my main box, the number indicating the size, the bigger the smaller. The other two had been #12s as well. To the One Fish, the Cahill should look from below pretty much like a Hornberg, similar color anyway.

The Cahill floated by the rock and the One Fish went for it with gusto. But, thanks to him or me or both, again no hookup. I observed that while I was mildly frustrated, interest and determination eclipsed that feeling. I was very focused, like an athlete (one with slow reactions) in the zone. On the second drift, the One Fish poked it again and, goddammit, wouldn't you know, I missed him again. Nothing on the third either. And so it went for a few more casts. We had ourselves a trend.

Next it was a Dark Hendrickson, a gray mayfly. My leader was getting a little bit short, so I invested an extra minute in replacing it. This was a fairly new leader; normally I would have tied on three feet of tippet because, as I may have mentioned, I'm cheap, and a leader costs three or four bucks. But, a Blood Knot for a new tippet is a bit involved, and I wasn't sure the One Fish had time to wait for me. I did take a moment to roll up the old leader neatly and slip it into the packet from which the new leader had come, to be pulled out for later reuse.

"Come on, let's dance, baby," said I to my foe. Sure enough, the One Fish took a run at the fly. In fact, he took two. And twice again we failed to consummate the relationship. This had gotten really interesting.

As I laid a third cast down, I almost didn't want him to hit it. We had a thing going. After the third cast, the Hendrickson wound its way towards the rock, accelerated around the side, and just as it hit the downstream edge of the rock, finally . . . nothing, bupkis, zilch. Yeah, I have gotten to know this guy!

For form's sake, I gave it another couple of tries—playing my designated part—before tying on a Royal Wulff (named for legendary fly tier Lee Wulff). It's one of the most beautiful flies, with its signature red band, brilliant white wings, and fox-colored hackle. How long could we keep this going, I wondered, as I tied the Wulff to the tippet. How long could I keep throwing new flies at the One Fish and getting exactly two hits?

Soon enough I had my answer: twenty minutes. Four different dry flies, and the One Fish was done. Never touched the Royal Wulff. I half-heartedly tried an Elk Hair Caddis and a few more patterns, but it was evident that the One Fish had figured out that someone was messing with him. He was probably still there and maybe still hungry, but caution trumped his desires, and he wasn't to be fooled. That day anyway.

Soon I moved on to the next hole with whatever I had on my line when I finally left the One Fish to his business. Oddly, the whole encounter was hardly a disappointment. On the contrary, it is one of my most memorable fishing experiences. For one thing, it made a good story. (Right?) And "I got eight strikes" sure beats "unproductive water." Most importantly, I felt great to really have a handle on what was going on below the surface of the water. Made me feel like I knew what I was doing, empty creel notwithstanding.

Guy is so good in part because he is, at heart, a scientist. Every cast is an experiment. There's theory and hypothesis behind the choices a good fisherman makes. Yes, you're trying to catch a fish, but the higher calling of your cast is to test your hypothesis about trout behavior under current conditions. Try to change just one variable at a time. The reason you cast the fly is because you think that standing here and sending the line over there to land just so with this fly drifting along that shore with a little twitch here and there . . . just might lead to a strike. If it works, good on you, mate! If not, you'll be smarter next time, and in the long run you will take more fish.

It's easy to feel like a genius when the fish are biting. The One Fish helped me see that just catching fish can be a hollow victory. I felt pretty smart after my twenty-minute lesson. The true joy of fly-fishing is figuring it out. A fish on the line is just a symptom.

That was the lesson of the One Fish.

Doug's Rock

By David Van Wie

Doug stands on a big rock in the sun, with every ounce of concentration focused on the tiny artificial fly in his fingertips. The sun glints off the flowing water several feet below where he is standing, shimmering in bright paisley patterns on his tan shirt, vest, and waders. Polarized sunglasses guard his eyes against the bright light, and a floppy-brimmed canvas hat provides additional protection from the late afternoon sun.

The fly that is the object of his attention is a tuft of tan elk hair tied securely on a hook about the size of the small end of a paper clip. The elk hair partially covers a wrapping of feather, so that all together the elk hair and feather look like a caddis fly, with the hair imitating the wing down the back of the bug, and the feathers poking out to look like the legs.

Doug patiently threads his translucent leader into the eyelet of the hook. From a distance it looks like he is rubbing his fingertips together. Once . . . twice . . . finally on the third try the thin line passes through the eyelet, and Doug wraps a few inches of leader around in several loops to tie the fly on snugly. Finally he is ready to present this fly in the pool next to the rock. "I hope this one is more successful than the last five," he thinks to himself. One of those five is snagged somewhere in the willows on the bank behind him, the result of a backcast that went a bit too far.

The rock under Doug's feet is about the size of a small car. Picture a Volkswagen Beetle sunk in the river up to its windshield. He is standing on the roof of that car while water flows past, several feet deep, with currents and swirls around the smaller rocks nearby. But this car is made of New Hampshire granite, not sheet metal, with sparkles of water droplets, tiny quartz crystals, and blotches of lichens instead of a fancy paint job.

A distinct pool, maybe five-feet deep in places, is filled with rocks the size of beer coolers and basketballs. The faster current enters on the side of the pool nearest to Doug. The far side of the pool is shallower, sloping to a pebbly beach on the inside of the bend in the river. The rock where Doug is standing forms part of the outside bank where the water hits the rocks before turning ninety degrees to the right.

Doug plays out his line, checks for tangles, then casts just fifteen or twenty feet upstream to let the fly dead drift back into the pool near his feet. He wants to float the fly on the edge of the main current so that it drifts between the quick water and the quiet water. On the third cast, after just five seconds of drift, a quick splash explodes under his fly as a trout is fooled by the ruse. He quickly lifts his rod tip, feels the trout vibrating the tight line for a second, then two, three—then it's gone. Having shaken the fly, the fish disappears like a shadow to the bottom of the pool. The fly and slack line dangle, waiting for Doug to pick up the line and try again. And so goes the next hour, as Doug works the pool with nymphs, dries, and streamers until the sun dips beneath the fir trees.

———

Halfmoon Beach, Hand on the Rock, Sam's Lookout, and Finnson's Cliff are a few of the locations in the Grant that have official names on maps. Who decided on these names is unclear to me, but I suppose it is the prerogative of mapmakers to convert the oral tradition of nick-naming places to publishing them on paper.

In the absence of official place names, The Boys have created our own names for some of our most frequent fishing spots. The Pool of No Luck on the upper Dead Diamond is so named for obvious reasons, a few notable exceptions notwithstanding, including Norm's biggest trout ever. We still call it the Pool of No Luck even though it is more accurately the Pool of Occasional Success.

Doug's Rock is named after my brother. It is on a bend in the Swift Diamond River, not far from the Management Center cabin. The Swift has a tendency to warm up rapidly during the day, so from late morning to evening, the trout prefer staying deep in the bottom of the pools, hidden in the gaps between rocks where the deeper ground-water flow is the coldest. Whether due to persistence, stubbornness, or a fisherman's focus, Doug would stand on that rock for hours trying different flies to coax the trout from the depths. He never wanted to leave that pool until he had caught at least one, insisting it was the only place he knew where there always were fish.

Doug was one of the earliest members of our annual fishing party. He hasn't joined us for almost ten years for tragic reasons, a tough story to tell. Yet his name has stuck to the place, partly because of his absence, but also because that was where he spent much of his time while he was at the Grant. We have all fished there, but over the years it became known as Doug's Rock. For me, Doug's Rock has taken on a more personal meaning, as a symbol of the burden Doug has carried for most of his life, a burden that has as much do to with luck and choices, good and bad, but also the harsh reality of the world we inhabit, even when we try to "get away."

———

When Phil suggested the first fly-fishing trip to the Grant, I immediately thought of inviting Doug, my younger and only brother, because I was looking for a way to spend more time with him, and fishing was an interest I thought we could share. Doug and I first trekked to the Grant during spring break of my senior year at Dartmouth. We skied in to Peaks Cabin and then Alder Brook Cabin with my dog, Bosco, a Lab-husky mix, pulling our gear in on a sled. We had a great time. So it was natural to invite him along for a fishing adventure in the Grant.

Doug and I always got along well, but we were different in ways that created a gulf between us. A friendly guy with a sparkle in his eye, Doug usually preferred activities that involved internal combustion engines, while I preferred non-motorized pursuits. But there was something else. Something was wrong, and no one in our family could quite figure out what it was. Doug was Doug. He had his share of difficulties and often seemed out of kilter. My two sisters and I loved him, and we worried about him.

Despite his obvious intelligence, Doug had had uneven success in the classroom. If he put his mind to it, he could get an A in almost any subject, but he frequently got distracted, seemed disengaged. In high school, trying to get out of the house in the mornings, I practically had to drag him out of bed to the car for the drive to school. As he struggled through high school, he seemed troubled. Looking back, I know I sensed there was something wrong, that he carried some burden hidden in another world, but as a teenager myself, I had no idea what, and I was busy with my own adolescence. His struggles continued into college, with far too much alcohol and partying, and he dropped out his senior year to go to work in our dad's insurance office.

We sometimes joked that Doug was the "white sheep" of the family. While the rest of us had dark brown hair, Doug's was light, almost blond. (His is now as white as snow, mine more salt and pepper.) I looked for ways to overcome the gulf and build a stronger relationship with my brother, and time spent fishing seemed to have some potential.

As a birthday present sometime after I moved to Maine, I gave Doug a three-day fly-fishing class at L.L. Bean. He enjoyed it, even with no motors involved, so I thought an annual trip to the Grant would be a good way for us to see each other regularly. And it would give him a chance to hone his fly-casting skills.

My college friends welcomed Doug as a member of our group at the Grant, and he joined us most years for about a decade. But I sensed he never felt entirely comfortable, that he didn't quite fit in among my friends. Sometimes he would go off on his own, or take long naps in the afternoon, occasionally avoiding our free-ranging conversations in the evening. It didn't seem like a big deal, and I never made mention of it. Doug was Doug, and I was glad to have his company, whatever the terms.

————

The stark reality of Doug's burden became painfully clear in 2004, when we learned that he had been sexually abused as a boy and in his teen years. We found this out after he was arrested for molesting two boys himself, thus continuing a horrendous cycle that is all too common in these cases.

Doug pleaded guilty and at age forty-five was sentenced to ten years in New York State prison. He served more than eight years and is now out on parole and under close supervision. He will be a registered sex offender for the rest of his life, and will have an extended probation, making travel outside of his local area very difficult. Visiting the Grant is still out of the question.

Following his arrest, and during his sentence and therapy, Doug disclosed to my sisters and me the full extent of his hidden troubles. While he wasn't using it as an excuse for his actions (which he has fully acknowledged as tragically wrong), he told us about his own sexual abuse as a boy, starting at age ten—first by a teenage neighbor, then by a cousin, by an adult neighbor, and by one of my high school class-mates. The curse of sexual abuse is that the abused very often becomes an abuser. It is a terrible cycle. One thing I have learned, though, is that not all sex offenders are the monsters that the media portray. This one is my brother. And as much as I condemn what he did, I still love him.

Suddenly, with this new narrative, my siblings and I all had to revisit and reinterpret the past thirty years of our lives, as well as our relationships with Doug. With both our parents deceased, I found myself questioning what they might have known, or at least should have suspected. Doug's burden is shared by our entire family. My sisters, my wife, and kids all visited him throughout his incarceration and have done everything we can to help him get back on his feet.

Doug's life now is pretty spartan. He works at a low-wage job (he was lucky to find one at all), attends AA meetings and various therapy sessions, and has a strict curfew and limits on his activities. He has been working very hard at dealing with his issues and has been making great progress. By talking freely to us about his burdens and struggles, Doug has released his demons and has been able to open up to the world. As a result, he and I relate better now than in years past, although I don't see him as frequently as I would like.

———

I visited Doug late last winter at his home, and took him cross-country skiing at a place where we used to go as kids. "Let's go out to Grafton," I suggested.

"Yeah, I heard there are some good trails around the lake," Doug replied, "and the lake is probably still frozen. Can't remember the last time I was out to Grafton, probably snowmobiling a long time ago. I think my machine broke down up there once. My friend and I had to work on it till dark to get it running again."

He excavated his old skis and boots from the garage. They had spent nine years in storage, and this was the first time he had used them since then. He wiped the mildew from the boots and ran back up to his bedroom to find decent socks so he wouldn't get blisters. The weather was fairly warm for March, so we only needed windbreakers and light gloves. A bright milky blue sky allowed the sun to reflect softly off the frozen lake. Big patches of snow on the lake offered an alternative to skiing through the woods.

"These spring conditions remind me of when we skied at the Grant," I said. Doug's expression changed, with a momentary squint indicating that he was digging deep into his memory to see the comparison. "Yeah, but there was a lot more snow up there," he noted. "I remember sinking to my hips when I took my skis off after we stopped for lunch. That's not gonna happen today."

Doug was a little unsteady on his skis at first, but soon there was a huge grin on his face as his old rhythm and balance returned. He was enjoying the day in the sunshine, with the smell of damp pine forest and the sound of crusty snow under his skis. His sunglasses slid down his nose from the sweat dripping off his forehead. "This is awesome!" he declared, pushing his glasses up. "But I'm sure gonna feel it in my legs tomorrow." We both laughed.

———

Even though it was more than twenty years ago, I still remember that I caught my first fish at Doug's Rock on an Adams dry fly. Casting from the pebbly bank on the far side of the pool, I floated the mayfly imitation down the upper run toward the corner of the rock. As soon as my drifting fly reached the shadow of the rock, a fat, eight-inch trout snapped it from the surface and darted out into the current in the wider pool. A couple of minutes later, I had the shiny brook trout in my net, and released it back into the pool.

Suspecting there might be more trout in the shadow of the rock, I bounced my next cast off the side of the rock. This time it drifted just an inch or two before another trout, similar in size, took my fly for a few laps around the pool. I believe I caught a couple more that afternoon. That day, as on many others, luck was on my side.

Doug's Rock is still a favorite spot when we fish that stretch of the river. It is never a sure thing, but always worth a try. And with each visit, we wonder when Doug might come back to the Grant and take up his place next to that deep pool. Hopefully, he will have better luck when he does. Doug's Rock and those persnickety trout await.

Standing Waves

By Billy Conway

Guy was in the stern, and I had the bow. The Dead Diamond River, normally a slow, meandering stream, was churning in flood stage after a week of rain. We had rods but knew the fishing would be worthless with the water high and muddy as it was. A fast ride was consolation for not being able to cast flies at the evening hatch. So far it seemed like a good idea.

When we started out in late afternoon, our biggest concern was whether we could reach our takeout point before dark. We would need to travel four river miles in order to get home. But now, as we rode the Dead Diamond, resurrected out of her usual pokiness and surging past the gravel banks, we felt like The Wise Guys of the Grant. The canoe was flying, and I thought smugly of Phil, Bob, and Norm. Those Boys had gamely decided to fish, but were at this moment, I felt certain, watching their flies disappear in the murky water as they tried not to fall in and be swept away. A long time ago I learned that this is called hubris.

Guy and I chatted as we rode the river, feeling like voyageurs, like the Green Mountain Boys on the way to Fort Ticonderoga, like tough, competent men of the North Woods. But in life there are sometimes "uh-oh" moments, and ours came suddenly. We heard the problem before we saw it. It was the roar of water—lots of it—falling fast. As the canoe rounded a bend, the river narrowed before us into a gauntlet of drops over ledges, alternating with huge standing waves. It was the kind of chute you would never ride down on purpose, but we both realized with a sinking feeling that it was too late to reach the banks. We were already committed. Guy shouted, "Down the middle!" and that seemed like the best and only idea. There was no room to maneuver, and if we turned sideways things would get ugly fast.

So we plunged into the raging chute, both of us paddling madly to keep the canoe headed straight. I braced a knee under the bow, which was a good move because the first drop almost threw me out. Time slowed down the way it does in moments of crisis, and it seemed for a while that all would be well. We were keeping the canoe aimed ahead, and it fell straight across a series of steep drops. I caught alternating glimpses of standing waves and of the sky as we bucked up and down, but we were keeping the canoe upright. As we emerged into a pool at the bottom of the falls a few seconds later I felt relieved and proud.

————

But those sentiments were premature.

If we had had a spray skirt we would have made it, but the canoe had taken on too much water in the drops. Now as Guy and I tried to proceed, the canoe, like every canoe that was ever drawn in a cartoon, gently sank in slow motion beneath the waves while we, the Wile E. Coyote and Elmer Fudd of this particular scene, continued the frantic motion of paddling. It would have been great comedy except that it was real life.

The water was chest deep and so cold it took my breath away. I struggled to make my muscles work as the Dead Diamond swept us downstream. Guy and I grabbed the canoe and what gear we could and half swam, half stumbled our way over to the stream bank. In all the commotion I had managed to embed a fly hook deep in my palm, which meant I was still connected to my fly rod. Reflexively I bit the line in half and then pulled the free end in to retrieve my rod from the bottom of the stream. In semi-shock we thought about what to do next.

The bank was too steep to climb out of the canyon we were in, and the road home was on the other side of the river.

"I think we have to try to empty the canoe and keep going," Guy finally offered.

We struggled desperately for a minute to lift and dump the canoe, but couldn't get a purchase because of the current and the steep-cut bank.

"We'll have to bail out as much water as we can with our hands," he groaned, "then ride the canoe to some place where we can empty it out."

I looked downriver. About a hundred yards further on there was another series of rapids. They weren't as big as the ones that had sunk us, but they looked more than capable of swamping the canoe, and we would hit the white water within a few seconds of launching.

"How are we going to get through those?" I asked, pointing downstream. "They'll take us out in a minute."

"We have to try," Guy replied "It looks like only two waves. We didn't sink until we hit the third wave."

————

We knew we'd be in trouble if we sank again. The water temperature was in the forties; the air temperature was in the mid-fifties. We were soaked, and it was beginning to drizzle. I had been shivering uncontrollably since I climbed out of the river, but the shivers had stopped, and now I felt myself beginning to get sleepy and wanting to lie down. Hypothermia was coming on quickly, and I could feel my thoughts becoming confused. Guy seemed like he was okay, but who could tell? We didn't have a lot of time.

I actually thought about how embarrassing it would be to die this way, not having had the good sense to avoid our predicament or find a way out. I thought about my years in the Boy Scouts and "being prepared," about how some of my friends would secretly wonder how I could have been so dumb. But with a fear-induced jolt of adrenalin and some irritation at myself for thinking this way, I shook off my waking dream. We had to move now or this could be the end.

"Okay, we gotta go," I said.

We did our best to dump out the water and by scooping with our hands managed to get the canoe more than half empty. Then we both got back in, our feet sloshing in the icy water, and began to paddle.

There wasn't a lot of time to think. The canoe hit the next rapids, but instead of bucking up and down the way it did on the falls, it plowed straight through the rapids like the semi-submersible it had become. The tips of a few waves washed in, but we were now part of the river, not something foreign floating on top of it. Guy and I just tried to keep the canoe upright, as maneuvering was out of the question. Then, suddenly, we were through the rapids and still afloat—barely.

We teetered along for a half mile or so and beached on the first sandbar we came to. Climbing out of the canoe, we were both moving like tired old men. The cold had us hunched over, and we were able to move our limbs only in slow motion. Methodically we rolled the canoe over on the sand bar to empty it. Then we wrung as much water as we could out of our clothes. Both of us were wearing fleeces, and I kicked myself for not wearing wool. I hoped the fleeces were made out of some kind of advanced material that would keep us warm when wet.

We didn't tarry and promptly got back in the canoe to continue downstream—both still alarmed but not speaking about our situation. Dusk was coming on; we were cold and moving so slowly. If we hit another set of falls—well, it probably wouldn't go very well.

But at just the right time, the Dead managed to help the living. The river widened out such that even in flood stage it was moving sluggishly. We were no longer being swept along and began to paddle to make up for lost time. Five minutes later the exertion of moving the canoe had warmed us up, clarity of thought began to return, and it was almost like our misadventure had never happened. We were still damp and uncomfortable, but everything was fine.

"Guy," I opined, "I do believe we dodged a bullet back there."

"Yep, that could have ended badly."

"What the heck was that place we went through?"

"Sid Hayward Ledge, I think. Hard to tell in the high water."

"*Sid Hayward?*" I couldn't believe it.

Sid Hayward Ledge was a gentle, sylvan glade, a place where people could swim and trout sometimes rise in limpid pools. But I thought of the ledges that formed the place. Then, in my mind's eye, I added a torrent of water, maybe four times the ordinary flow of the river, and, yes, it looked about right. Good Lord, what had we been thinking when we got into this canoe, and why hadn't we thought about those ledges and their funneling effect?

———

The rest of our descent of the Dead Diamond was uneventful. We paddled through the dusk, got to my car, then picked up Guy's car, loaded the canoe, and headed back to Sam's Cabin.

It was completely dark when we reached Sam's, and The Boys were relieved to see us. The high river and late hour had them worried. Guy and I told our tale of adventure and near miss, and then it was time for dinner.

But for me getting back to the cabin still left one remaining problem to be solved: the fishhook embedded in my palm. Under the dim mantles of the propane lights in our quarters I took some forceps and experimentally wiggled the hook to see how much it would hurt to push it through my skin. It would hurt a lot. The hook was in deep and not budging. I considered my options. Maybe I could just leave the hook in until I got back home? But in that case infection was likely. On the other hand, the nearest hospital was probably forty miles away, and I'd be gone half the night if I went looking for medical help.

"Any of you guys have any ideas about how to get this hook out of my hand?"

The Boys crowded around to take a look.

"How about pushing it through?"

"Hurts like shit, and it's in too deep."

————

"I can get it out," Guy said after giving it a quick check.

"Tell me."

"I learned this trick from my buddy Lou. You tie a string around the bend in the hook. You push the shank into the skin. Then you yank on the string, and it pops right out."

I thought about this for a moment. "Guy, you sure that works?"

"Yep. I've seen it done. When I hooked Cheryl's arm one time."

"How come it works?"

"I think it's because when you push the shank into the skin, it changes the angle of the hook so that the barb doesn't catch on flesh when it's being pulled out."

Guy was not a bullshitter and almost always knew what he was talking about. It would probably hurt a lot, but that was okay if the hook came out quickly.

"Let's do it."

Guy produced a shoelace and carefully tied it around the bend in the hook. I pressed the shank of the hook into the skin of my palm (which did not feel great).

"You ready?"

"Yeah." I gritted my teeth expecting the worst.

"One, two, three . . ." Guy yanked hard on the shoelace and the hook came right out, making a little pop as the skin dimpled around the barb and then let go. Much to my surprise it barely hurt.

"Wow, Guy. Outstanding. That was remarkable."

————

Later that night as we were all getting ready to turn in, Philip, who doesn't hand out compliments that often, sidled up to me and said, "Hey, I think you were pretty brave about that hook extraction."

"Yeah?"

"Yeah, definitely."

Huh. I got into my sleeping bag and began to think about the day's events. It probably would have been better if Guy and I had managed to make it through the waves without sinking the canoe. Less drama and more competence. My self-concept as an outdoorsman was offended. But still, we had kept our heads and managed to cheat death just a little bit. And to be told by one of your closest friends that you've been brave, that was something, too.

"Well," I thought, sleep coming on and my mind drifting between far-off galaxies and the woodsmoke smell of the cabin, "I think I'll have to remember this day."

Late To The Party

By Ed Baldrige

M y history at the Grant is a little different from the rest of The Boys. I was a few years late to the party.

I had heard of the Dartmouth Grant while an undergraduate, but it always had this faraway and inaccessible aspect to it. While attending one of our class reunions, I heard some of my former rugby teammates mention that they were heading to the northern New Hampshire wilderness for some fishing and camping after the reunion. I was intrigued but didn't ask any questions.

Fast-forward ten years, and I was fishing in the Rangeley Lake region of Maine where I ran into a local guide who mentioned the Dartmouth Grant as a nearby fishing spot he really enjoyed. With 28,000 acres of wilderness and beautiful rivers, he told me, it was also one of the last places in New England with a native brook trout population. The cabins were only open to the Dartmouth family and their friends, but his brother was an alum so he visited every chance he could. I decided I would schedule a trip for the following year.

I went through the usual channels of reserving a cabin and securing keys for the gate and began the process of rounding up folks who might be interested in a fishing trip. I first approached some Dartmouth friends who had never been to the Grant. Their responses were generally, "sounds like fun—except for the fishing and the bugs."

I cast my net a little wider, as it were, and after emailing Guy a few times for info, finally arrived in the Grant with a relatively new friend. This fellow, the self-proclaimed Wall Street God of Restructuring, was an avid fisherman and was just back from a guided trip in Patagonia catching huge brown trout. Another friend from my trading days in New York arrived with canoes and coolers strapped to his SUV, along with a retired oil executive from Texas. He also had invited a person he barely knew, a Maine Guide who had recently won the Maine champion flycaster award.

Things got a little clunky, as they sometimes do in a small cabin with people who aren't close friends and have different ways of approaching the wilderness. The Wall Street fellow mentioned more than once that he didn't get many days off and needed to catch more and bigger fish. "Where else could we go?" he kept asking. I really wanted to stay in the Grant, but he persisted.

The retired executive and his Texas friend were more or less there to scout the property. The Texan also complained about the lack of fish and the abundance of mosquitoes and no-see-ums as he flogged the water with his rod. The Maine Guide busied himself telling stories of loves lost and found as well as his numerous exploits in the fishing world of Maine.

Things were not going as I had envisioned.

After dinner on Saturday, the Maine Guide decided to visit the cabin across the road. I guess he thought he'd find a better audience for recounting tales of his fishing experiences and what he knew about the Dartmouth Grant, even though this was his first time there. I later learned he had walked in and made himself at home among a group of fellows who were totally confused about who this teller of tall tales was and why on earth he'd chosen their cabin to visit. Eventually, I wandered over, too.

When I walked through the door, however, I was amazed to see a bunch of familiar faces, the same guys who, years before, had spoken so reverently of the Grant. Until then, I had no idea we were all there on the same weekend. The Maine Guide finally left, and I stayed behind with the Dartmouth '79 crew. Everything suddenly felt right for the first time all weekend.

For these guys, the concerns weren't who got the biggest fish or even how many fish everyone caught. Their conversations were directed, it seemed to me, at the bigger picture of life as well as the quiet and solitude afforded in the Grant. This was how they rekindled their friendships every year.

Ever since I officially joined The Boys the next year, the Grant trip has become a special pilgrimage for me. I find myself opening up to these guys about challenges in my life that I rarely share with anyone. At the same time, I have come to realize that all of us have faced challenges along the way with our careers, marriages, families, and health. For a few days every year we catch a few fish, drink a few beers (a lot less these days) or maybe sip a little scotch, and we share a camaraderie that is fortified by our times in the Dartmouth Grant. I came late to the party, but am glad to be a part of it.

The Make-up Trip

By David Van Wie

Making the turnoff from Route 2 toward Grafton Notch in Maine is my favorite part of the drive to the Grant. The road through the Notch is twisty and very scenic, and there is rarely any traffic. I like to push the speed a bit, but watch carefully for moose and other wildlife. This is definitely moose country. And bear country. And deer country. You have to keep a watchful eye on both sides of the highway here.

The road climbs gradually through Grafton Notch State Park and continues to Upton, Maine, before descending past Lake Umbagog and on to Errol, New Hampshire. In the summer I have made the 28-mile climb to Upton on my bicycle. You feel tiny next to Old Speck, Maine's fourth highest peak, at 4,170 feet, towering on the left, and the cliffs of West Bald Pate on the right. The road is steep near Screw Auger Falls and on up to Moose Cave and Mother Walker Falls, then more moderate but steadily rising over the pass to Upton. The view across Lake Umbagog from Upton is brief but vast, with the Diamond Peaks and the Dartmouth Grant twenty miles to the north. Almost there.

This particularly memorable trip I made to the Grant was not in June, but in mid-September. With chilly nights in the Mahoosuc Range, the leaves were turning with more color every mile as the climb continued. I could feel that we were in for some classic autumn weather this weekend. Northern New England doesn't get any better than this.

This was my first trip to the Grant in the fall, a new and welcome adventure. When I got to the gate, I immediately noticed the lack of mosquitoes, a sharp contrast to the buzzing onslaught that greets us there in June.

After passing the Gate Camp, I always stop on the Perley Churchill Bridge, high over the Diamond River. The flow was low but

130

sufficient for fishing. Happy to be free of the Gorge above, the river charges over rocks and boulders in a wide open valley, carved clear of trees by the massive ice flows from upstream that gouge the channel anew each spring. At midday the colors from this vantage point were a laser light show of reds, oranges, and yellows set off against the dark green of spruce and firs.

The air was crisp and inviting. I rolled down the windows on the drive to Merrill Brook Cabin, inhaling deeply the smell of the woods and the turning season. I couldn't wait to get set up in camp and out on the water to see what fall fishing was like at the Grant.

This was a special trip, one we have since dubbed Phil's Make-up Trip. When he was unable to join us in June, we had promised him another chance to enjoy the Grant, and I was only too eager to make the "sacrifice" of coming back in September.

————

June 2009 was our thirtieth class reunion, arguably our best one ever. Our reunions are special because the Dartmouth Class of 1979 is an extremely tight-knit group within the broader cadre of Dartmouth alums—almost cult-like, but in a good way. And Phil—who long ago was elected Class Mini-Reunion Chair for Life—is a big reason why our class is so close-knit. He is and always has been a family man. So it's not surprising that he has worked hard for years to make our class feel like a family. And he's good at it.

That June, our plan was to go up to the Grant immediately following the goodbyes of reunion weekend. Rather than our usual Thursday to Sunday stint, we modified the plan that year to Sunday through Tuesday to give the fishermen from afar a break on travel. A back-to-back reunion and Grant trip seemed almost too good to be true. And so it was.

The reunion was remarkable, not so much for the numbers who could attend, but because of the quality of the relationships of those who did and the richness of the activities planned for us. My favorite event was a panel discussion called "Reinventing Yourself." Several class-mates spoke of career and personal changes in their lives, how they dealt with and embraced changing careers, started a nonprofit organization, or reoriented their lives to focus on different priorities or new activities.

After the panel presentation, the discussion around the room became very personal as people opened up about events in their lives—divorce, second marriages, forays into politics, and writing music, among them. The sense of brother- and sisterhood was palpable. Conversations continued for hours after the panel was over. It was cool. We felt like family.

Sometime on Saturday afternoon, Phil came to me with a worn and worried look. No, it wasn't a hangover; something serious had changed his demeanor. "Shit, Guy, I have to bail on the Grant," he said. "This totally sucks, I know, but I want to go home to help Beth. We have been having some big-time teenager issues lately, and I can't let Beth deal with this alone right now. She just called, and I need to go help her work things out."

I knew how much this was killing him. All of The Boys try to plan our entire year around the Grant trip. He wouldn't miss it except for something dire, but that didn't make it much easier for him. The situation at home was going to be a tough slog. But he had made the right choice.

"Philip,"—I actually call him Philip much of the time—"you gotta be there with them. It definitely won't be the same at the Grant without you. But we understand." I quickly thought to assure him that he wouldn't have to skip a whole year. "Look, we'll plan a make-up trip for later in the summer or the fall. We'll get you up there somehow so you don't miss a year. Not the same, for sure, but something you can look forward to."

A little later I spotted Norm across the reunion tent and wandered over to let him know what was going on with Phil. He understood immediately. We all have kids, and we knew we'd all make the same decision without hesitation, although some of us might whine about it more than others.

"Hey Nerm, I am thinking of a make-up trip for Phil. Maybe in early September. It'll be a bit cooler, and no bugs. What do you think?" Norm's response, raising his beer cup to mine with a plastic clunk: "I'm in."

The June trip after the reunion ended up including just four of us: Norm, Klingon, Bob, and me. We had a good time as always, winding down after the hubbub of one long party. But the trip felt out of joint without Phil. We caught some nice fish, ate and drank the usual fare, and had a great time reminiscing not only about our past year, but also about the reunion. It was a fine time at the Grant, just not quite what any of us would have preferred.

Phil went home to take care of his family. Inevitably there are tough times in our lives as parents. When things go askew, it can feel like our world is falling apart. Our hopes and dreams for our kids suddenly seem so fragile. Fortunately, in Phil's case, things worked out okay.

Phil and Beth weren't the only ones to have endured a bumpy patch. A year later, my son and his now notorious crew of friends known as the "Thirsty Thirteen" got into some trouble from a school party. It was a growth opportunity for him in the long run, but at times like that, we realize that there are many ways for our plans to unravel in a hurry. We realize that, as our kids grow up, we have less and less control over their lives. At some point, all we can do is cross our fingers. We become coaches. We provide advice and hope that they listen. Sometimes we beg them to listen, while knowing that we were young once and learned hard lessons from stupid mistakes. As our kids grow into young adults, we set whatever boundaries we can to demonstrate our principles. We pick our battles. But we never stop worrying.

The Boys of the Grant are all dads. Proud dads. Very proud dads. We love our children and each other's children. We want what is best for our kids, and spend time sitting around the table in the cabin agonizing over whether we are pushing too hard, or getting too wound up. We share stories, successes, struggles, and strategies. At the Grant, we try not to get caught up in bragging about our kids, but that's nearly impossible.

All of us have been fortunate to have kids who have given us great joy. Sports, scholastics, loving relationships, and family fun are the topics of many conversations between the fishing tales we share at the Grant. Even though we are away from our families for the long weekend (and thankful that they indulge us so), we sure spend a lot of time talking about them. The Grant trip is really about sharing our lives and family experiences, while catching a few fish here and there. We aren't away from our families. Together, we are family.

———

Up at the Grant that September, the stress was gone. Unless losing a fly on your backcast counts as stress. Or burning the bacon. Phil, Norm, and I were thrilled to be back in our refuge.

The rivers look quite different in the fall adorned with leaves turning radiant colors. The red maples change first. Various shades of crimson, orange, and yellow reflect off the pools, as fallen leaves float by in the current in the full spectrum of the autumn forest. Damp, dying leaves and spent pine needles give the North Woods a different smell than we are used to in June: a mix of the heady balsam aroma and the moist, slightly mildewy smell of the leaf drop.

We had to dress for the chill, with extra layers and long sleeves. In the morning and evening frost, we stoked the wood stove in the cabin, adding the smell of wood smoke to the air and to our clothes. The change of season from our regular June trip was a sensory extravaganza.

We fished Sid Hayward Ledge and many of our other favorite spots. With just three of us, we stayed together, fishing and chatting within ten or twenty yards of each other. The Pool of No Luck was not only scenic, but productive for a change. Norm hit the lottery with a fat and colorful fall trout.

I took a few smaller trout from the run above the pool, casting to the far bank and retrieving back to the shallows on my side of the run. In this glide, I often try to "paint the water" with a small streamer or wet fly, running my fly across every square foot of the run until I find where the trout are holding. Once I see a rise or a flash at my fly, I switch to a dry fly and try dead drifting it down to the holding spot, hoping for a strike. In the fall, a big high-floating fly, like a Royal Wulff or a Kauffman Stimulator, may do the trick. And then there's the time-proven Elk Hair Caddis.

We loved the autumn conditions. The sharp air and low water brought new mysteries to solve. We welcomed the challenge.

———

A rare shot of Phil (L) in waders with Guy and Norm (R) at Merrill Brook Cabin on the Make-Up Trip.

Midway through, we realized the trip was also a serendipitous mini-reunion of freshman-year hall buddies from Cohen Hall. Later, we all lived in Richardson Hall—me with Phil in a double, Nerm in a single down the hall. I am willing to bet this was the first time just the three of us had hung out together since 1976. Mr. Mini-ReunionChairForLife had done it again!

The best way to summarize our fall trip is by quoting from the entry we left in the cabin logbook:

> Our first fall fishing trip to the Grant, after 15+ years of trips in June. Coincidentally, the maiden fall trip was to the same cabin as our maiden June trip many years ago, which started a cherished tradition of annual trips.
>
> This was a "make-up" trip for Phil, since he could not join us in June due to some family priorities. We didn't want him to miss a year, so Norm & I promised a fall trip. Phil has been the heart and soul of this tradition, so missing a year would be unthinkable.
>
> As for fishing, Phil took the prize, taking eight on Thursday and over a dozen on Friday (we released them all). Everyone caught enough to feel some well-deserved pride under challenging low water conditions. A mixture of sun, a rain shower, a front blowing

through, and more wind made it interesting. We hope to add a fall trip to our annual plans, as one trip per year is never enough time in the Grant.

The Best Arrival

By Phil Odence

I 've arrived at the Grant a couple of dozen times, always eager, always smiling. The best arrival was several years back. For whatever logistical reasons, the others were delayed getting to LL Cote and Norm and I headed north before anyone else had arrived. We pulled up to the Management Center and hauled in our gear. Having roomed together in college and respecting each other's snoring capabilities, we aimed for bunk rooms at opposite ends of the cabin.

I always pull my sleeping bag from its stuff sack first thing to let it fluff up, and while I was in process Norm called from the living room.

"Philip, there's a bottle of Jack Daniels on the table half full."

"Yeah, baby," was my response.

"And there's a note on it," he continued. "'A gift for my friend Phil Odence.'"

"Yeah, yeah, sure," said I, ever the skeptic, while fluffing my pillow.

"No really, I'm not kidding . . . 'for my friend Phil Odence, from your old dean, Ralph Manuel'."

I strolled back out into the living room. Yup, sure enough. It was a note from Ralph N. Manuel (he never advertises that the N stands for Nixon), Class of '58, dean of the College our freshman year and throughout our undergraduate tenure. Perhaps the last of the Old School administrators at Dartmouth who (thankfully) understood that boys will be boys, or so I learned having met with him a few times to work through a few, let's call them challenges, with the rugby club. I have a number of wonderful memories of Ralph and his wife, Sally, who also once saved my ass with a plate of food the time I drank too much while bartending at a faculty cocktail party.

So what's with the whiskey? Well, we'd had a number of classmates up to Hanover for Winter Carnival the previous winter and ambushed

Dean Manuel at the hockey game for a picture with all of us. I'd stayed and chatted with him a bit, and we inevitably got onto discussing the Grant. Frequently, our trip coincides with his (now forty-years-standing) annual trip, and when I run into him at the occasional Dartmouth event, fishing usually creeps into the conversation, including the episode of the Fallen Soldier. Ralph knows I'm tickled by his favorite saying, "The worst glass of bourbon I ever had was terrific!"

Somehow he had logged in the dates of our trip from that conversation and figured out that we were taking over the Management Center the day his group left. And evidently this occurred to him as he went to pack up the bottle of Jack. The penny dropped, and instead of stowing the bottle, he left it, labeled with a Post-it note for me to find, and in doing so forged for me a lasting memory. That was it. The best arrival ever.

Of course, now that I think of it, the worst arrival I ever had at the Grant was terrific!

Oh, Deer. Watercolor & Ink by Phil Odence, 2004.

Tenkara

By Ed Baldrige

At the Dartmouth Grant, each of The Boys has simplified the fishing experience in one way or another. No one arrives with an SUV stuffed with equipment, and most of us have streamlined the rod choice to one or two, the fly selection to a few favorite patterns. Some have traded the waders for the absolute minimum, sneakers and shorts, and others limit gear to what they can fit in their vests or chest packs. All of us are trying to re-energize ourselves by unplugging our computers and iPhones and plugging into nature.

Tenkara is my way of simplifying.

Traditional fly-fishing came hard for me. The learning curve was relatively steep, so I went at it like the multidisciplinary sport that it is: I studied fish visuals to determine which size tippet to use in certain waters, balancing visibility with enough strength to hook the fish; on the stream, I learned various styles of casts and when to mend the line upstream or down. But the goal appeared to be about casting long distances with the proper rig, not catching fish, and I wasn't getting much better at either. I went through a series of guides, lessons, seminars, books, and videos, and I bought loads of equipment. The problem was that every time I went fishing with a more experienced fly fisherman, I became overwhelmed with choices: flies, line types, rod selection, strike indicators, and so on. Finally, when one instructor started teaching about insect life cycles, I had a hunch there must be a simpler way. When was a guy supposed to get a chance to just fish?

I'd read some of Patagonia founder Yvon Chouinard's writings on management and learned on his Wikipedia page that he is "particularly fond of tenkara fly-fishing." After some surfing, I stumbled on Chouinard's 2009 *Fly Rod and Reel* essay "Simple Gifts," in which he writes about the ancient Japanese fly-fishing method that has only recently been practiced outside of the mountain streams of Japan. He describes fishing with tenkara equipment he'd received as a gift years before and how it helped him dial back his gear and his fishing techniques to just the basics. The bonus was he caught more fish.

Former banker Daniel Galhardo had barely launched the website for his new company, Tenkara USA, when I called him to buy a fly rod. The rod telescopes to between eleven and thirteen feet and uses a light line about the length of the rod, three to six feet of tippet material, and a fly. It reminds many people of fishing in farm ponds with a long stick, some line, and a hook. Original tenkara rods were bamboo. Nowadays they are made of graphite. There is no reel, and the rod collapses to about twenty inches. The entire fly-fishing outfit weighs less than three ounces and fits in a daypack. It is also remarkably effective.

In a word, tenkara clarified my fishing experience. I began to spend more time fishing and less time fussing with strike indicators, selecting flies, or worrying about how much weight to add to the line. We joke that with tenkara things get "reel" simple, and meanwhile I never have to hear the word *mend* again.

––––––––

Ed, alone among The Boys, favors the Tenkara method of fishing on the Swift Diamond River. Photo by Bob Chamberlin.

There is some ramping up with tenkara and some differences you need to get used to. There's a much different technique involved than with traditional fly-fishing, and you need to get closer to the fish. A few steps closer. Without a lot of fly line, you have more direct contact with the fly. You can sense the activity around it. The fly rod is really light, thin, supple—and therefore sensitive. You can actually feel the fish grab. Compare that to a regular fly line: a fish can strike and spit out the fly before you know it's happening. As your tenkara technique improves, your catch rate goes up.

Everyone knows that successful fly-fishing is mainly about presenting the fly to the fish. Tenkara provides all of the necessary components, including a relatively long, drag-free drift without any line on the water. It allows you to pinpoint the fly in small pockets, over or around cross currents, and under banks that are difficult for Western fly fishermen to reach. Most importantly, the fly spends more time in the water.

Many tenkara anglers, following the old traditions, simplify things even further by using only one fly pattern for all of their fishing and have learned how to camouflage that single fly by varying its behavior. In most cases the fly pattern is some variant of a wet pattern called a *sakasa kebari*, which uses a reverse hackle to give the fly a lot of movement in the water. The same fly can be manipulated to sink like a bead head, skitter on the surface like a caddis, or drift it like a wet fly.

When I fished with Gelhardo, the entrepreneur who started the tenkara movement in the States, and with Dr. Hisao Ishigaki, one of the better-known tenkara anglers in Japan, both used only one or two fly patterns for all of their trout fishing, and both were remarkably successful in crystal clear creeks with easily spooked fish as well as in fast-moving mountain streams with hungry trout. (The Grant has both types of water.) Once, during a fishing trip in Utah, I watched Dr. Ishigaki, who is relentless, fish the entire pool I was about to fish in the time it was taking me to select a fly. He did it with a single fly, which he had tied on in about fifty seconds.

The truth is, I don't fish tenkara all the time. I do notice, when I fish the "regular" way, that I bring a lot more stuff, which, frankly, is sometimes a comfort: I won't be without the right fly. In keeping with the ethos of tenkara, I force myself to take less—maybe a small box with five or so flies. I haven't been brave enough to limit myself to one. I'll need better technique before I get there. And even though I may have been an early adopter, I'm not much of an evangelist. I don't think any one of The Boys has yet taken me up on trying tenkara.

When I reach for my tenkara fly box, I only have a few patterns, mainly in the simple kebari style: black or brown thread, hook size 12 or 14, with those reverse hackles moving in the water. Sometimes it's a relief to have less. And sometimes I still have to remind myself that brook trout are not the smartest fish in the world, and if I concentrate on techniques and fish where the fish are, I'll have a good day on the water.

Boys, Wine, and Bullshit

By Phil Odence

Wine has played an increasingly important role in the non-fishing part of our trip. A little over a decade ago, it cracked into the previously exclusive beer club as a fitting adjunct to Saturday night Bucatini Amatriciana, the spicy pasta recipe I brought to the trip as an alternative to chili or Bolognese. In a brilliant flash, Guy was inspired to cart along a jug of Woodbridge Cabernet one year, and the rest is history.

Billy soon discovered that he could avoid flak for never doing the dishes by assuming the role of team sommelier, and so instituted a yearly stop at the state liquor store in Hooksett, New Hampshire, en route from the airport to the Grant. Soon, out of deference to his own leanings and our modest budget, our trusted wine steward began generously self-funding a special bottle or two each year, a "Clos du" this or a "Grand Cru" that, the virtues of which he would extol to the unwashed masses. And thus did wine evolve from being a one-time pasta pairing to an integral component of the trip, as well as a subject of conversation and, ultimately, debate.

When it comes to wine appreciation, The Boys line up something like this: Billy, Klingon, Ed, Guy, Bob, Norm . . . and good ol' Philip, the scale ranging from poser to philistine. I can't say for sure, but I might be the Phil in Philistine. (Maybe that's why Billy calls me a philistine—in the nicest way possible— which he has done more than once over the years.)

When those at my end of the scale speak of wine, they say things like, "I like it!" or "Mmmm, good Pinot" (about a Merlot). Billy and his lot will describe a red wine as "agreeably complex with nuanced jammy notes of cassis, apricot, and chocolate and a balanced, yet silky tobacco finish." I hyperbolize; he's not really that pompous, and neither am I so imperceptive, but there's no question we regard and approach wines very differently.

The debate is whether it is all bullshit. Is a $500 bottle of wine fifty times better—or any better, for that matter—than a ten-dollar bottle of Mark West or a jug of Woodbridge Merlot, and can you even tell the difference? The philistines certainly lean towards, "Yes, it's bull, and no, you can't really tell the difference." And the tonier Boys believe in their palates enough to think it was a wise investment to lay out $750 for a case of something a decade ago and set it aside to mature.

Over the years, our conversations evolved until eventually we hit on the idea of a blind tasting. And so it was that in 2012 we resolved to try our palates at playing connoisseur—swirling, chewing, and sniffing with the best of them. Billy and I, as poles in the debate, loosely committed to organizing the Great Tasting of 2013.

————

We are not a terribly competitive lot when it comes to fishing, but The Boys do enjoy getting each other's goats now and then. So, my thoughts that year leaned toward how to "win," how to beat Bill at this game. Looking back, I must have lacked some confidence in my conviction, or else why would I have thought about how to cheat? No, *cheat* is too strong a word, but I did contemplate how to tilt the test table a bit. After all, there were rules to be formulated. Why not make sure they favored my position?

Several of the staff at Gordon's Fine Wines & Liquors in Waltham, Massachusetts, where I live, are wine savvy and helpful. I sought assistance there once when I needed a bottle that would favorably compete at a company party as having the funniest label. One of Gordon's employees spent ten minutes walking me through their extensive selection, which, oddly, did not happen to be organized by degree of label humor. And so, one slow night that winter I went back in and described the proposition at hand to Gordon's chief buyer. How would he set it up so as to have less expensive wines shine? What varietal would allow a modest wine to fare best? What should be the price threshold?

The advice I remember most clearly was to steer clear of Pinot Noir. A cheap Pinot will actually include only a scanty percentage of Pinot grapes and is therefore easier to distinguish from an expensive, pure Pinot. He was confident we could get a pretty good Cab for twenty dollars, and so suggested we focus on that varietal and set the threshold at about twenty-one dollars. For whites, he thought the straightforward nature of a Sauvignon Blanc would work in my favor and that I might find a good New Zealand entry to compete with the French bottle my adversary was likely to select. The wine expert and I were both, at the time, assuming this would be a one-on-one smack down, with me purchasing the Rocky Balboa and Billy popping for the Apollo Creed.

But it didn't end up that way. With a week to go, Billy volunteered to manage the whole thing and, out of convenience, I agreed, even relaying information I'd gathered at Gordon's, as well as *Consumer Reports* ratings I'd been researching. And so, Billy did it all.

Like envelopes at the Oscars, the brown bags Billy carted in to the cabin that June were properly sealed and stashed in the corner of the Management Center kitchen awaiting the great event. He shared that he had bought four Pinots (the dreaded varietal) and four Chardonnays. Thursday would be red night.

————

Wine tasting, it turns out, has been a subject of debate not confined to The Boys of the Grant. A little web research will turn up a surprising number of articles strongly questioning the wine emperor's clothing. One article, "Wine Tasting is Bullshit," is particularly scathing as is one in the *The Guardian* called "Wine-tasting: It's Junk Science." A somewhat less pointed piece entitled "Does All Wine Taste the Same?" was published in *The New Yorker* on June 13, 2012, within days of the debate that led to our tasting explorations. Only after our tasting did I come upon that report and found that its conclusions were similar to (though not nearly as insightful as) my own.

Most of these articles cite common sources ranging from well-known anecdotes to highly controlled scientific studies. Generally, the punchline to all of the investigations is that wine tasting is highly subjective, random, and inconsistent. One oft-cited study fooled experts into extolling the virtues of a glass of red-dyed white wine using adjectives reserved by the elite for reds.

You'll also find, via Google and a few wine magazines, frequent mention of the famous Judgment of Paris, an epic wine competition.

This well-known wine tasting has little in common with the Greek myth of Helen's abduction and how it triggered the Trojan Wars, though the use of the myth's title is a clever pun. The upshot of the tasting was that a panel of eleven (mostly French) judges in France chose a Stag's Leap Cabernet as the top wine on the planet, legitimizing California in the eyes of the wine world for the first time. That story doesn't really suggest that wine tasting is bullshit, just that French wine snobs are full of bullshit. And that California has some pretty good wines.

Though few experts condescend to react to the ravings of the hoi polloi, you will also come across rebuttals like "This Piece About Wine Tasting Being Bullshit Is Bullshit," which appeared in the web magazine *Bullett*. When they do condescend, they do so with great condescension. Such authors typically take the backhanded, highfalutin position that if you can't taste the difference, you should not spend your hard-earned centimes on a bottle worthy of only a sophisticated palette. Drink what you like—and what you can afford. Lah-dee-dah.

After our first tasting, we read and shared these pieces. As far as I know, none of The Boys were exposed to these biases prior to the first Judgment of the Grant. Even I tried to enter our tasting with an open mind.

————

The big moment arrived soon after we'd cleared the dinner dishes. This time Bill had a good excuse for not washing the dishes, as he was setting up at the east end of the Management Center's mile-long table. We averted our eyes as he assembled four clusters of three "glasses"—irreverently, we used red plastic cups—labeled #1 to #4. We were all to log our own reactions and eventually transfer them to a matrix for scoring. Scoring was a simple "low point" system. We were to rank the wines 1 through 4; the one with the least total points would win.

Some rules had to be fashioned on the fly: Did we drink serially or in parallel? Were we allowed to talk and discuss? Billy more or less officiated as we all decided it was okay to talk about the process and the flavors, but not about superiority or rankings. We shuffled in around the end of the table and began, most of us starting with #1. We tasted, and then nibbled on crackers before moving to the next cup.

Everyone's first reactions were similar: "Oh my God, this is hard!"

Some wines were similar. Some were more distinctive. None jumped out as either brilliant or awful. Holding four flavors in your head is tricky. Clearly there was no clear answer after one round. Any thought of competition was gone; we just wanted to figure this shit out.

We swirled and chewed and swished our way through another round. Someone, after a small taste of #4, reached diagonally across the table for some #1 and observed, "I'm having a very difficult time telling these two apart." I concurred, and then it crossed my mind that Billy, the devious bastard, might have doubled up the same wine in #1 and #4. More of the conversation was about the experience than the wines. "Wow, is this interesting." "I keep flipping back and forth between a couple of favorites." "There was one I didn't like as much the first time, but now I think it's my first choice."

I imagine this is an unusual focus for discussion at a wine tasting, though perhaps not so unusual as where this tasting was taking place, deep in the New Hampshire woods. You ask Robert Parker, Jr., about the wine, not about how he grew with the experience of tasting it. But The Boys being The Boys, we tend towards the meta. Everyone rose to the occasion; the posers weren't posing. The heathens were doing their damnedest to get it right. Jointly we strove for an interesting outcome. And got one.

After tallying the results, Billy nodded, confirming the intriguing story only he had seen unfold, and then did a great job walking us through his slow reveal. Wines #1 and #4 were the ones we thought were similar. Out of the brown paper bag, Billy produced a bottle of Acacia A and a Banshee Sonoma, both decent, middling wines he'd selected at the New Hampshire state store. We'd each ranked them close to each other, and on average they scored about one position lower than the other two, yet-to-be-revealed vintages.

"Okay, so I stacked the deck a bit," admitted Young Conway as he slid the next one from the anonymity of its bag, "with a Chambertain Clos du Beze." French, I surmised, from Billy's perfect pronunciation—his having grown up in New Orleans where the language is actually useful. It was a 2006, as we came to know, a banner year for Pinot Noir grapes from Bourgogne. And it was a particularly good year in the *Appellation d'origine contrôlée Côte de Nuits*, a subregion evidently so special that Napoleon would drink no other Burgundy.

It was a bottle Bill had hand carried from home that had been in his collection for several years. You'd pay about $200 for that bottle today. And, if you were like me, you would comment profoundly, "I like it," which I did. It was distinctive and delightful. I'd had a tough time deciding, but ended up ranking it a close second. And it ranked, on average, just a few tenths of a place below the yet unrevealed winner.

I examined the Chambertain's label, a little in awe of the $200 price. The label could not have been more classic in appearance. Its stark French text—black, gray, and a little burgundy, in a beautiful all-caps font—against a slightly creamy white background bespoke Old World elegance.

———

"And now, our top-ranked bottle," pronounced Conway. He looked more like a fisherman than a sommelier, as he fished out the last one. The bottle was soft shouldered, similar in shape to the previous, but capped by a fat plastic-topped synthetic cork.

In obvious contrast to the Chambertain, the label on the bottle Billy now set before us was clearly the handiwork of a contemporary graphic artist. After a pause, during which we could only hear some large insects banging against the window screen, Conway announced the name, delivering the punch line with the flair of a perfect cast, ". . . the Pepperwood Grove Pinot Noir." And so did the label proclaim, in a hip-looking sans-serif font above an abstract design. The clean, flowing graphic gave the impression of a hillside, doubtless decked with vine rows, which were suggested by a spectrum of green graphic waves ranging from near-black rifle green to a pale pastel. Completing the picture was a subtitle that read: "The Groovy Green Bottle."

Pepperwood Grove, an offshoot of Sebastiani based in Sonoma, processes Pinot Noir grapes sourced in Chile's Central Valley. We all agreed the result was pretty groovy. It received several #1 rankings, and Billy, himself, had rated it second only to the Clos du Beze. Its lowest rank was a third from Klingon.

"The Acacia and Banshee were calculated selections," Bill told us. "This one, I grabbed off the shelf randomly from among several ten-dollar Pinots." He had, in fact, paid eight dollars for the Pepperwood.

Yes, the intriguing outcome of this, our first tasting, was powered by dumb luck. Billy could easily have grabbed another wine that likely would not have fared so well. We came to learn that Pepperwood, in particular this varietal, was widely heralded as an amazing best buy and a very good wine regardless of price.

———

Our modest tasting pours had left more than half in each of the bottles, so there was plenty of good wine left to drink, and we stood around continuing to sip a little of this and some of that. Here was the really interesting thing. Unconsciously, for me at least, we all gravitated to the Chambertain, and drained the bottle in the next ten minutes, leaving most of the Pepperwood in place. What was going on here?

This behavior supports some of the more charitable tenets of the wine-tasting-is-bullshit columns. The concept is that you can't separate a wine's other attributes, not even price, from its taste. The gestalt of a glass of wine comprises the label, the setting, the karma, the beautiful creature across the table, and, yes, even the price. The experience of drinking a $200 bottle of wine surpasses that of drinking the cheap stuff. (But, evidently, only if you *know* it cost $200.)

We've traded articles on the subject since. It's worth some Googling. You'll also find similar discussions that go beyond wine. A Spring 2015 article in *Bourbon Empire* sparked some discussion among The Boys about the tricks the whiskey industry plays on us, essentially marketing the same mass-market swill at higher prices under different names with descriptors like "small batch" and "craft" and touting old family recipes.

In my late teens, I organized a New Year's Eve beer tasting. My best memory is of a vocal, self-proclaimed Schlitz hater, who blindly thought the masked Schlitz I gave him was St. Pauli Girl and gave it top marks. Upon learning of the embarrassing result, he proclaimed, "I don't give a damn, I still hate Schlitz." It's something Klingon might have said, and I like that about Klingon.

I recently came upon a relevant podcast from *Freakonomics Radio*. There's a particularly good segment about a bunch of haughty, wine-enthusiast Harvard Fellows being fooled in a tasting set up by Freakonomist Steve Levitt. The story concludes that when it comes to taste (with regard to all the senses), people rely too heavily on the subjective opinions of experts. Levitt says, "It's a wonderful gift to like cheap food." I feel that way about wine. It's rare for me not to love a glass of red wine and also rare for me to spend more than fifteen dollars for a bottle. That said, I'd be a little embarrassed to show up at a dinner party with an $8.99 price tag on a bottle. So, I always scrape them off.

The following night in the Grant, after we returned from the streams, we tasted Chardonnays with enjoyable, though less dramatic results. A cheapo white earned a couple of good rankings but overall ended up in the cellar. I was one of the likers, but I don't drink a lot of whites, so I'm prepared to believe educated palates were more perceptive in that case.

A year later we repeated the test. Predictably, though I don't think anyone actually predicted, Billy stuck a Pepperwood Grove into the mix again. And guess what? It ranked in the middle. Guy says he's continues to buy Pepperwood and finds it inconsistent. Perhaps he's right. Or perhaps it just depends on the night and the setting and the karma.

For me, the most interesting wine of Year Two was a red that I initially thought tasted like shit, literally. It turned out to be a vintage of good repute. We discussed this one, in depth, after the rankings, and I learned from my more refined brothers that "earthy" is a more positive way to say "like shit." A number of the guys really liked it. Through the discussion, they actually coached me into pulling a 180. Once I appreciated the character of the wine, acquired the taste I guess, I came to like it. The more we talked about it, the more I liked it.

My wife would be shocked to hear me acknowledge the value of talking about things. The Boys enjoy discussing all kinds of stuff:

Fishing, of course. . . Wine, Women, ditto. . . Maybe next year we'll do Song.

Dog Days

By Bob Chamberlin and Phil Odence

In May of the year our family got a new dog, the question arose: should I bring him to the Grant? No one else brought his dog. Each had their reasons. Norm didn't have one. Phil's dog would likely be consumed by larger local fauna. Billy, Ed, and Klingon flew in to Manchester . . . too complicated. DVW (as I refer to Guy) has a dog, and he lives relatively nearby, but he asserted that April, his Lab–bluetick-hound mix, would be off like a shot the instant she sniffed the wild air, perhaps never to be seen again.

I was never much of a dog person, but the kids asked and I agreed and that's how Bogie became a beloved member of our family. He was a big dog, a retriever-shepherd mix with good stick-to-the-master's-side instinct. So, yes, I would bring Bogie. I didn't even ask.

Within the first minute of our arrival Billy and Bogie formed a close bond. DVW was less enthusiastic. Truly a dog lover, DVW has a farmer's practical perspective on animals and their places in the world, and he was skeptical about how Bogie would affect cabin life and the fishing.

Bogie soon endeared himself to all by the grace with which he endured a fly hook in his ear, the result of a clumsy cast of mine. I think it was an Adams Dry, but no matter. What mattered was that the hook was barbed and deeply embedded, frustrating our efforts to free it. In the next few days, we made multiple attempts to extricate the fly. Billy was especially sympathetic, having been through the embedded-fly thing himself, but we had no success. Extraction would have to wait for our return home and a visit to the vet. What stuck for the long term was the memory of the errant fly, my convulsive casting, and Bogie, The Boys' Best Friend.

Not long thereafter, poor Bogie encountered further calamity when he jumped an Invisible Fence at our home in Vermont to attack a passing lawn-service trailer. Something about rattling noises riled him deeply. The trailer won, and Bogie paid with his right front leg. No more trips to the Grant for tripod Bogie. A few years later, he departed for the great fire hydrant in the sky, but is remembered as a loyal fishing companion.

Recently, I took in a rescue dog named Jack, a Napoleon of a pup: Jack Russell terrier–black Lab mix with a large spirit in a twenty-five-pound body. Once again the question was raised: should I bring my dog?

This time I asked Phil. His response was something like, "Sure, okay, whatever, just don't mention it to Guy." I sold myself on the idea by emphasizing Jack's good behavior, his need for affection, and his sure destiny to win hearts. I was warmed by the vision of introducing Jack to Billy, imagining the inevitable, immediate friendship.

———

So it was that in June 2015 Jack came along in my Subaru for the drive to the Grant. We were the last to arrive at Sam's Cabin. As I recall, the arrival was unspectacular. There was a hint of fawning from Billy, but nothing overdone. Jack was a bit surly at first, as is his habit with new people, especially men. However, it didn't take long for him to become integrated into the scene.

I celebrated the uneventful arrival by removing Jack's collar, festooned as it was with various tags, which I feared might irritate The Boys with their jingling. Included among the jingly tags was a round Petco.com cheapie, on which was inscribed JACK and my cell number. I was anticipating Jack's romping stream side as Bogie once had and was concerned that the collar might hang up on a stray branch or downed limb.

After a couple of days of rain, the rivers were running high. With a light mist still in the air, we decided to hit the upper Swift near the Winter Road for our initial foray. We hoped that the trout would be holding in the pools and pocket water upstream in the watershed, where there would be less water. We piled into two cars, Ed with Klingon and Norm in a yacht of a Suburban; Phil, Billy, and DVW with Jack and me in the Subaru.

Jack settled into Billy's lap in the back seat. DVW, in the front seat, leaned over and asked something like "Does Buddy-Boy know his way around here?" I remember clearly the term "Buddy-Boy" as well as the implication that we were far from the sidewalks and parks of Burlington, Vermont, Jack's and my hometown.

Arriving at the Winter Road, we disembarked and began the ritual act of setting up our rods and blessing the flies we each tied onto our leaders. Meanwhile, my canine sidekick darted in and out of the underbrush, drawn by thousands of new scents, but he frequently trotted back to the cars and around our feet.

Jack was fifteen months old, an adventurous teen in dog years, but like his predecessor, he had developed a wonderful willingness to stick by me. By and large, Jack would stay on my heel walking around Burlington. With some vigilance, I even managed to keep him from chasing squirrels. Likely in the strange, wild surroundings of the Dartmouth College Grant, he would be too nervous to stray far from Dad.

Once our gear was set, we dispatched into three groups: Norm and Billy heading upstream along the grassy road; DVW and Klingon heading downstream; Phil, Ed, and I splitting the middle. Phil was drawn to tiny, but rushing Alder Brook, which joined the Swift just up from the fork in the road.

As I was retying my boot, Jack followed his new friend Billy a couple hundred feet up the road. As I stood up, Billy turned and yelled something to the effect of "Keep your dog close to you." So, I called for Jack, who enthusiastically charged back to my side.

The banks of the Swift are a thicket, wild with tall reeds and alder brush. We bushwhacked toward the river with Jack following in my trail, an effort for him in the tall grass. To our surprise, the bank was fairly clear as we reached the Swift, and Jack seemed to cheer. I, on the other hand, was discouraged with the roiled and rushing waters. It hardly seem worth stepping in, so I stayed perched above on the bank and got the line out with some short backcasts, carefully avoiding the trees and Jack's ear.

————

"Any luck, Philip?" Bob asked me as he and Jack emerged from the chin-high foliage.

It was a pleasure to report that Alder Brook had produced a six-inch trout, presumably the first one of the trip for our team. But after fishing the brook's one accessible pool for awhile, I made my way back and into the Swift, careful not to get swept away in the raging water. I'd been working along the shore for a short while when Bob and his dog arrived.

Bob was captivated by my incredible story of angling success and probably by the artistry with which I was flicking my Muddler across the torrent. Just as I was getting to the exciting part of my story, we became vaguely conscious of a rustling in the weeds between us and the road. "Jesus, I hope a great horned owl doesn't swoop down and make off with Jack," said Bob.

"Guy would say it's God's way of telling you not to bring house pets to the North Country," I rejoined before going on with my tale. A few minutes later, though, Bob abruptly froze with an "Oh, shit" look. He called and whistled for Jack. Nothing. "I better get him back here," he said, making his way through the tall weeds toward the cars.

I kept fishing, but stayed within a couple of rod lengths from the shore. The water was running hard so I half-heartedly tied on a black Woolly Bugger, hoping to get it down in the current. Nothing was happening, and I concluded that I'd worked this water for too long. I joked to myself that it was time to go help Bob rescue Jack. Little did I know.

All the others had given up on the Swift earlier than I did. Back near the cars I encountered Guy and Klingon, driving in the wrong direction. No, I'd not seen Jack. I explained where we'd been and that it couldn't have been more than five minutes later that Bob went off to find his dog. It was now clear that Jack was really lost, and The Boys were in motion.

The Daves had driven back towards the Confluence, thinking perhaps the dog had headed "home" for the cabin. Bob was hiking the Winter Road in the opposite direction, while Ed, Billy, and Norm were driving up towards Ellingwood Falls, shouting and whistling along the way. They had planned to fish until Bob emerged at the other end of the gated road, which is really a marshy path that is sometimes plowed for logging trucks in winter, hence its name.

Because an army marches on its stomach, Guy ran Klingon and me the mile or two back to Sam's Cabin to get dinner started, then headed back to rejoin the search. As we set up the grill, Klingon and I were muttering things like, "Not good. Just come back with the friggin' dog, guys, come on." As dusk turned to darkness, the gang returned, dog-less. Bob was hoarse from yelling, and the mood was a little strained.

Resigned that we'd done what we could for the night, our spirits were buoyed somewhat by a fine meal and drink. But the conversation kept coming back to poor Jack, particularly as the rain that had started as we took the chicken off the grill intensified. Billy mused on the nighttime perils a dog might face, and we debated their likelihood. Norm wondered if Jack might follow our scents back to the cabin.

Conversations out of Bob's earshot were more pessimistic. The big fear was that Jack might have gotten on the trail of some wild animal and could by now be anywhere across thousands, *tens of* thousands of acres. He might eventually emerge but it could be miles and days away. Where would we start?

Klingon suggested that we head back to the Winter Road and build a bonfire to attract his attention. We weren't convinced a fire would actually be visible from too far into the woods, nor that it would necessarily attract him. And it was raining like hell now. Poor Jack; not a lot of insulation on his wiry frame to stave off the chills.

We also talked about a grid search first thing in the morning, but how much grid could seven guys manage? Then Klingon had a stroke of brilliance. If our morning search was unproductive, we'd cart the grill from Sam's Cabin down to the fork at the Winter Road and grill up burgers for lunch. Surely a dog's nose would pick up the aroma for miles. Worst case, we'd have burgers for lunch! With that hopeful thought in our heads and Klingon's Johnnie Walker in our bellies, we headed off to bed.

Early the next morning, as the rest of us were dragging our sorry asses out of bed, Bob was out flagging down a logging truck at the intersection. The loggers were sympathetic and promised to keep their eyes peeled. Bob returned just as we discovered that Guy had mistakenly bought whole coffee beans, with no way to grind them. This provided comic relief; had poor Bob been the culprit we all knew we would feel badly about busting his chops, per usual, over this grievous error. Instead we were able to cheer him up with the observation that Guy was almost as bad at shopping as he was. Guy wasted no time, though, in procuring a couple of flat river stones, a large bowl, and strainer, and proceeding to hand grind the North Woods' Finest Stone Ground Coffee. It was only slightly grittier than normal.

Over Guy's breakfast sandwiches, Bob laid out the plan he'd

hatched during a restless night. His strategy was to spread the word as far as he could to leverage more eyes and ears than the fourteen sets we could bring to bear. He would make signs to put in all the cabins and at stores in town, call the local vet, and basically alert everyone he could from Errol to Wentworth's Location. Bob had resigned himself to the long-term play, figuring Jack would turn up eventually, but maybe long after we'd all returned to the real world. Everyone offered to join him (the fishing would suck anyway), but Bob resolved that his sign plan was a one-man job.

Soon after he drove off, I got antsy. I grabbed Billy and we jumped in the Jeep to go back to the soggy scene of the crime. On the way out, we gave the couple staying next door in the Management Center, a heads-up about the lost dog. Helen Lukash (Class of '78) and her husband, Peter, wished us luck in our search and promised to keep an eye open.

———

Downing my cup of North Woods Stone Ground, delicious as it was, did not bring me out my black hole. Visions from a sleepless night still haunted: a coyote, a raptor, other real predators had all gnawed at my consciousness as I tossed the night away. I even worried about the mosquitos buzzing my poor Jack's ears and his pink underside and feared the hard rain would push his lean body towards doggie hypothermia. Fighting despair, I somehow found the energy to launch my mission.

I set out for Errol and LL Cote to procure materials for signs. I would also phone some folks—the Dartmouth Outing Club, police, firemen, and who else?—to let them know that a small dog was lost in the very large Second College Grant. Would they care? Who would help?

As I drove towards the Bridge below the Confluence, I spotted a work crew of ten or twelve Dartmouth students cutting next winter's firewood for the cabins and rolled down my window to share my plight. Sympathetic responses from around the circle assured me that Jack had these guys on his side.

Continuing on my way, I flagged down a few more loggers heading into the Grant for the day. Once again, nods of understanding and the good feeling that Jack's Army was growing. Still further on,

I crossed paths with Lorraine, the Grant caretaker. She knows everyone and was keen to disseminate the news. Not yet out of the gate, I was already feeling as if my efforts might pay off.

On the road to Errol, I continued to build the search party, signing up the keeper at the Mt. Dustan Store, two soggy roadside walkers, and the staff at the US Fish and Wildlife Center for Lake Umbagog. Desperate as my effort felt, all these people buoyed my spirits with their commitment to help find Jack.

Finally, I pulled into the Errol Library, which has an Internet connection, but it was closed. Damn. No matter, I carried on to LL Cote to pick up the sign materials. There were plenty of choices, and I came away with bright fluorescent stock. Using my best attention-getting script, I wrote over and over: LOST DOG, TWENTY-FIVE-POUND BLACK LAB MIX, LOST EVENING OF JUNE 21, SECOND COLLEGE GRANT. I included my contact info, hoping that someone would find him and then find me.

When I was done, I posted the bright-colored signs all over Errol. Okay, there isn't much *to* Errol, but I had it covered. While I'd been at LL Cote, the locals directed me to possible points of cell reception on Highway 26, a couple of miles south of town. So, I headed there to call the Outing Club and Dori, my girlfriend/roommate/partner. Dori is more or less Jack's mom, and she was great. She calmed me down and offered all sorts of helpful suggestions. Only later did I learn how devastated she was hearing the news.

After making my distress calls, I headed back to Sam's Cabin, and when I arrived, The Boys were all outside accompanied by some new faces. Burr Gray (Class of '79) and his daughter Rachel ('15), who had just graduated, were going to stay at Hellgate that night and had stopped by on their way in. I scanned the yard for the hopeful vision of prancing little black legs, but was disappointed.

"Any news?" I asked.

————

With Bob off on his mission, the situation we were facing, combined with the unusually high waters, provided little motivation for any of us to rush out onto the river and fish. Besides, though chances were slim, wouldn't it be great to be a hero and save the day—and the dog? Billy and I were engaged in scant conversation as we drove out the Swift Diamond Road in my Jeep.

Hopeful, but with grimly realistic expectations, we pulled up to the head of the Winter Road. It was only a stone's throw from the spot I'd last heard Jack rustling through the weeds. I am known for having a hell of a whistle, but neither my toot nor Billy's shouts brought any reaction from the dark woods.

After a short jog up and down both roads, we climbed back into the Jeep and proceeded towards Ellingwood Falls. Every few minutes we stopped for a shout and a whistle, but ultimately arrived at the falls empty-handed. After the previous night's drenching rains, the rushing waters on either side of the road were particularly loud and spectacular.

Could Jack really have come this far? If he had, would he have hung around? "Jack! Jack!" Could he even hear us over the roar of the falls? Crap. On the way back we hardly bothered to call out any more. Not that we'd given up, but we had certainly already covered this territory.

We were discussing plans for fishing the upper branches of the Dead Diamond, to the extent we thought fishing might be possible, when—"Holy shit! That's him!" We both erupted almost simultaneously.

An instant earlier, my brain had registered a smallish coyote springing from the steep road bank about fifty yards ahead. But it was no coyote. Jack stood there in the road like a gunslinger staring us down. I stopped the Jeep. Opening the doors sent him scooting back up the bank and into the woods. As we moved closer, Jack was surveying us from above, darting back and forth along the ridge that paralleled the road. "Here Jacky-Jacky!"

So, there we were, in a standoff with the nervous little dog, not a hundred yards from the place where he disappeared eighteen hours earlier. And now, try as we might to coax him down, he just stared and yipped back at us but refused to come any closer.

As Billy had developed some rapport with Jack, we decided he would stay on the scene while I'd drive back to Sam's Cabin on the off chance that Bob had returned. Worst case, I would be able to fetch some aromatic foodstuffs to augment our personal charms. But before I got into second gear, I spied Billy in the rearview with a bundle of dog in his arms.

With the towel I kept stashed in in the rear, we dried damp, shivering Jack, and soon he was wrapped snugly on Billy's lap as I drove straight back to the cabin. Once there we couldn't find his proper food, probably still in the back of Bob's Subaru, so I scrambled some eggs and mixed in some leftover rice while Bill related our account to The Boys. Taking no chances, we kept Jack securely inside the cabin awaiting Bob's return.

Sitting around the picnic table enjoying the sun that had burned off the mist, we celebrated with a late morning beer. Soon Bob bounced up the road, back from his mission to Errol. Spontaneously I hatched a quick plan: "Everyone keep a straight face. Billy, you go inside."

We're twisted but not cruel, so we kept the good news from Bob for only a couple of minutes while he told us of his adventures. Then Billy emerged from the cabin with Jack at his side, and Bob could not believe his eyes. "Nooo, you've got to be kidding me!" was his delighted and delightful reaction.

I was snapping photos of the miraculous reunion and kept the camera in front of my face to obscure my teary eyes lest The Boys discover just how sappy I really am. Reuniting man and dog instantly lifted what could have been a pall over the whole weekend.

Late that afternoon I felt some more tears of joy when we came back from searching unsuccessfully for fishable water above Little Garfield Falls to find a grocery bag on the cabin steps, inscribed "For Jack and The Boys." Helen and Peter from next door had left us a present of Jack Daniels and dog biscuits, an unsavory combo, but perfectly appropriate to the occasion. Our gracious neighbors had seen Billy and me drive in with Jack, and it inspired this thoughtful gesture. So touched were The Boys that we invited the couple to our wine tasting that night, and they were eager and pleasant participants.

And we all lived happily ever after. Just in case the question comes up again: Sure Bob, you can bring your dog. No harm, no foul. Just don't lose the little bastard.

City Boy

By Norm Richter

At a cocktail party last year, I fell into conversation with two men, longtime natives of the Chicago northern suburbs. We were standing in a crowded corner near the bar, the only ones drinking IPAs and eyeing the meager supply left in the cooler. Among other things I have learned about the Midwest is the fact that very few of those born and bred here seem to have a taste for either spicy food or strong beer.

These two had a clear appreciation for hoppy beers. I know this isn't a defensible litmus test for identifying guys likely to be interesting. But I stubbornly believe it creates a presumption. Life rewards the ability to work out shortcuts. Call it beer profiling. In any case, we three were certain to account for the couple of six packs of Lagunitas India Pale Ale among all the Coronas and Bud Lights.

"So, where would you want to live, if your job didn't make the decision for you?" asked Jay.

"Well, you're one of those outdoorsy guys, so you wouldn't want a city," said Mike.

I looked at Jay to see how he would respond, but he looked at me the same way.

Mike had meant me. I couldn't believe it. *I* was the outdoorsy guy? I laughed. Me, the New York City public school kid who showed up for the three-day Dartmouth freshman hiking trip with only black jeans, black T-shirt, and a toothbrush. Me, who spent summers before college, when not working odd jobs, on hot asphalt basketball courts or concrete schoolyards playing stickball, and who didn't learn to swim until I was fifteen. Me, who at age twelve could do three bus transfers to navigate Queens and get to Shea Stadium, but who at eighteen thought that those splashes of blue paint along the Mount Moosilauke hiking trail were the work of backwoods vandals.

Norm shows his tight loop casting technique at Slewgundy.

It was mostly the Grant that transformed me, turned me into the "outdoorsy guy" that those IPA drinkers in Chicago took me for. After college and law school, I lived in Washington, DC, for twelve years, working for the three branches of the federal government and in a law firm. Aside from short hikes along the Potomac River, that Moosilauke freshman trip had been pretty much the sum total of my outdoors experience.

I met Pam in DC, and we were married on Block Island, the small chunk of land about fifteen miles off the coast of Rhode Island. This was where Pam had spent all her summers growing up. Fishing was built into the bones of Rhode Island, where razor-toothed bluefish boiled the water in feeding frenzies each spring and fall, competing with the young striped bass.

We settled in Providence, on the shores of Narragansett Bay, where I was able to keep a boat near my home and get out onto the bay to chase those bluefish and stripers. Sea salt was gradually replacing the asphalt in my bones.

I was pleased but hesitant when Guy and Phil invited me to join them in their budding tradition of fishing at the Grant. I'll be the comic relief, I thought. A fish out of saltwater. So I read some books. (Pam would have asked someone for help, but I reached for the literature.) I ordered a beginner fly rod from L.L. Bean and practiced in my front yard. Not that it helped.

My first trip to the Grant I recall as a time spent untangling line from tree branches and losing flies to snags every ten minutes. This was costing me about ten dollars an hour in lost flies alone. I struggled with impossible knots for attaching tippet to leaders and flies to tippet, and complained that the only beers available—in a world of emerging American craft beers, for Chrissake—were Buds.

———

As can happen when you discover enjoyments later in life, these days I'm all in. But also, as happens when you come late to a skill, I'm painfully aware I'm no natural. The sun is fading, the midges are swarming around my face, and rises are suddenly everywhere. Working upstream from the bridge, I squint at the larger insects fluttering up from the water. The rises become more urgent. A small brook trout actually leaps clear of the water in a flash of silver and orange. My Hornberg is of no interest. "Match the hatch, match the hatch," I mutter, having memorized the mantra.

That's the moment you fish for, right? The Zen moment when you tie on the right fly, present it in the perfect way, and immediately feel the tug on your line that says: "Yes, you get it, you are one with the forest and the stream and the trout, Little Grasshopper."

So on all-too-frequent occasions like this I ask myself: "What would Guy do?"

Laugh at me, probably. No, actually, he would not. Because he is a good guy, Guy (I always *wanted* to juxtapose those two words!) would patiently tell me what he was using to pull those mutant-size brookies out of the same water that I just thrashed unsuccessfully for an hour. Then I would try that fly, but with no better luck than before. It worked when certain conditions existed. And now only something else will work.

See? Zen-like life lessons spontaneously combust around fly-fishing. Fish where the fish are. Piss before you put on your waders. Watch your backcast.

———

Now I live in Illinois, and the trip to the Grant involves an airplane. I miss the travel from Rhode Island, driving in the Jeep Wrangler, Philip's or mine, as the sun comes up. From Providence, up to Boston, around Route 128 to fetch Phil in Lincoln, and give a quick hello to a sleepy Beth while fending off the excited dogs. Stopping in Carlisle, Massachusetts, at the general store/bakery for coffee and scones. Driving over the New Hampshire border on Route 3 as the fog and early morning chill begin to burn off, then taking the top down and shouting at each other over the wind as we pass through Concord, New Hampshire, and finally see the buildings thin out and the mountains rise up as we head up I-93 along the flank of the White Mountains. On one trip the Jeep was engulfed by a herd of 200 Harleys, riders with big bellies and streaming white hair, headed for the annual Laconia bikers' convention.

We'd stop for gas and savor the laconic New Hampshire comments (is that why they call it Laconia?) as the man behind the register makes change. On through Littleton, past the historical marker in Stark for the prisoner-of-war camp where captured German U-boat crewmen were held during WWII. Passing the red covered bridge over a rushing stream, we check our phones one last time as the last bars fade out, and we go offline.

———

Pam and I and our daughters now live just north of Chicago. No terrain higher than the chair you're sitting in. Drive an hour in any direction and it doesn't look much different. Near where I work, there is a microbrew pub proudly called Flatlanders.

Midwest people are good people, and our time here has been good for us. Within walking distance of our house is Lake Michigan. You can't see to the other side, but if you could, you would see Michigan dunes rise up to rival any on Cape Cod. There are big fish out there. If you have a boat bristling with outriggers, heavy weights, and planers, the deep water of Lake Michigan can put on your hook a forty-pound Chinook salmon or a lake trout the same size. But as much as we like it here, we can't shake the feeling that our home is in New England. It is startling how the shape of the terrain shapes your sense of where you belong.

———

One day in the Grant, I stood waist deep in the Swift Diamond when there came a thrashing in the bushes along the bank. A moose blundered down the slope, skidding in the mud, and splashed heavily into the cool water. She was about five rod-lengths away. On her side was a large red gash swarming with black flies. She lowered herself into the cool, rushing water with evident relief. I stood stock still, waiting to see whether she would blame me for her troubles. Instead, she simply stared at me placidly, like a matron in a hot tub.

After a while I went back to casting. Under my breath, I said, "Lady, don't mind me. I'm just visiting."

Standing In The River

By David Van Wie

I 'm standing in the river casting and hoping we will see a hatch. Last night, their first night ever at the Grant, Phil and Bill Burgess fished at Slewgundy at dusk and hit an epic hatch—fish were rising and splashing everywhere. Beginners luck! Slewgundy is a series of deep pools above a small drop-off formed by a rock outcrop, or ledge, across the Dead Diamond River. They managed to hook a few fine fat trout by doing their best to find a fly to match the hatch.

But tonight, nothing is happening. Same time, same place. So it goes with fickle summer hatches.

———

I'm standing in the river, teaching Nerm and Klingon a few casting techniques. I am showing them a cross-body backhand cast, as well as a roll cast to use when the willows and weeds behind you are eager to steal your fly. Neither Norm nor Dave had been fly-fishing before this trip, so I try to offer a new trick when they seem ready. After only a couple of days on the water, both have been catching fish now and then, so they seem happy with their progress.

———

I'm standing in the river with a fucking song stuck in my head: "American Woman" by The Guess Who. Not a bad song, mind you, but after forty-five minutes I am tired of it. It could be worse. At least it is not "Whoomp! (There It Is)," which was all over the radio on the drive up.

I didn't even realize I had a song stuck in my head for the first twenty minutes, but once I noticed, it really started to annoy me. Cheryl calls this an earworm. I don't like fishing with worms—of any kind. If I were catching fish right now, "American Woman" probably would have

166

run its course. But it persists. I think the rhythm of my fruitless casting has now synchronized with the song.

I attempt to dislodge it peacefully by thinking of other songs to replace it. I try singing "Lay Down Sally" by Eric Clapton. Nope. Two or three casts later I am back at "American Woman." I try "Friend of the Devil" by The Dead (I am near Hellgate after all). That doesn't work either. So just before I am about to pound my head against a rock to make it go away, I remember a favorite old standby: "Fishin' Blues," a classic song from the 1920s by Henry Thomas that was later recorded by several artists in the '60s and '70s, including Taj Mahal. I start singing out loud, and it works like a charm. And it even brings some luck. I get a strike.

> Yes, you've been fishin' all the time.
> I'm a-goin' a-fishin' too.
> I bet your life your lovin' wife.
> Catch more fish than you.
> Any fish bite, ya got good bait.
> Here's a little somethin' I would like to relate.
> Any fish bite you got good bait.
> I'm a-goin' a-fishin', yes, I'm goin' a-fishin',
> I'm a-goin' a-fishin' too.
> —by Henry Thomas (1928)

———

I'm standing in the river, and my shoulders have tightened up because I've been out on the river for almost ten hours today. This is power fishing. With two young kids at home, I am very lucky to get a whole weekend to come up here. The Boys all feel the same. So we are going to fish every available minute.

But I am exhausted, and my whole body hurts. As I climb up the bank to head to the car, my aching back reminds me of a time a few years ago fishing with Lou, my fishing buddy in Maine, who personifies the concept of power fishing.

We'd been fishing since dawn. It was the fall spawning run, so we were on the river before first light to beat all the other fishermen to the best pool. Now the sun let us know it was past noon. We each had caught a few landlocked salmon and some nice trout, but I was hungry. Starving. And the muscles in my upper back and shoulders were in a knot.

As we walked back through the woods to the car from the river, our waders squishing in the soft sponge of balsam fir needles, I said, "Man, am I ti-yyyurd! My back is killing me. I am so glad I put that tennis ball in my bag. When we get back to the cabin, I'm gonna hafta roll on it for an hour to loosen up my back."

"Sorry about your back." Lou responded. "And it's good you have that tennis ball. But I am really glad that I arranged to have the Swedish Bikini Team parachute in to the cabin for the afternoon. While you are rolling around on that tennis ball, I will be getting a full body massage from the Sandersson twins."

"Okay, Lou. In your dreams."

————

I am standing in the river, and it is getting dark. It is after 8:30 and no longer light enough to tie on another fly. But I don't want to quit. Visions of a huge trout rising out of the depths in the twilight keep me going: a big mama that will fill the cabin with an unforgettable story over dinner. But the no-see-ums are making the backs of my hands burn like acid. Also, I am worried about wading in the dark, unable to see the rocks under the water when I walk back to shore. It was tricky enough wading in the light. I will have to feel each step carefully with my feet and hope I don't stumble and fall in, the water rushing into my chest waders. I'd rather not have to tell that story. Again.

I cast one more time into the dimly lit water, hoping the trout might still see the fly silhouetted against the sunset sky. Nothing. Finally, I stow the fly on the cork handle and head slowly back to the cabin. The other guys have been back awhile. The cabin will be bright and cheerful. There will be chili on the stove and a cold beer in the cooler.

As I climb the river bank, I see Venus low in the sky to the west and a scattering of other stars showing early in the darkened sky. It is going to be another spectacular night for stargazing in the Grant.

————

I'm standing in the river, at a bend in the Dead Diamond, just above the inlet of the Little Dead Diamond. A steep bank rises up behind me, covered in willows and weeds. Because there is no room to backcast, I am roll-casting a Royal Wulff, with a bead-head nymph dropper, across the river into a deep pool below a big rock. I had a strike on my first cast, so I am intent on getting another good dead drift when I hear a loud noise above me on the bank. My first thought is that Phil is playing a trick on me. I look up over my shoulder. It isn't Phil. At the top of the bank is a cow moose. She is peering down at me, and she looks pissed.

The bank is about ten feet high. It's another six or seven feet from hoof to furrowed brow. She is way up there, and she wants to come down. I realize now that the muddy path down the bank behind me is her path. She must come this way often, and I am in her way.

I apologize politely, and wade about ten yards downstream to the bottom of the pool. This is enough, apparently, as she immediately comes clomping and sliding down the path, splashes into the river and wades across to the other side. She casts a sidelong glance at me with one eye as she clambers up the bank on the other side and heads off into the willows. I decide to move down to the next pool, assuming the fish in that pool are probably as spooked as I am.

———

I am standing in the river barefoot. This June has been very hot. The Hellgate Hilton has been sweltering, especially in the evening with the gaslights burning. The walk down the path is like passing through a sauna filled with the warm damp smell of balsam and spruce. There is no perfume sweeter than this delicious scent of the North Woods. I love it, even when it is mixed with a touch of bug dope for good measure. It is late afternoon, and I have decided to forego the waders, cross the river in my sandals, and walk up to the pool just above Hellgate Gorge.

The bank where I am standing, the inside of a sharp bend in the river, is covered with pea-sized gravel. With each cast, my feet sink a little deeper into the gravel. After a dozen casts, my feet are buried above the ankle bone. They are also numb from the cold. This is a poignant lesson in how much colder the temperature can be at the bottom of the river compared to the surface. And it may explain why the trout have been sitting down there all day, ignoring my fly on the surface.

———

I'm standing in the river and my fly is snagged on a log under the water. After many years, I have finally learned to be calm when I get a snag. The worst thing you can do is tug and make it worse. The best thing to do is relax and think about options. I execute a nice snappy roll cast across and upstream a bit, pushing some of the sinking line to the far side of the log. When I start to retrieve, the fly-point backs out nicely from the log.

I haven't been catching any fish this morning, and a save like this may just be the highlight of my day.

———

I am standing in the river fishing naked. Yes, naked. And so are the rest of The Boys. For some damned reason, I thought it would be funny to get a photo of us all (from the back, mind you, and from a distance) fly-fishing buck naked. I suppose the idea was inspired by those funky fundraising calendars featuring the old ladies in the garden club, covered only by their hats or garden tools. Or something like that.

And for some damned-er reason The Boys all went along with it.

Backs to nature: four of The Boys pose for an unseemly shot of fishing in the altogether near the Management Center in 2002.

So here we are, all naked as the day we were born. We had to wade carefully out into the river below the bridge. We are all trying to cast without hooking each other in unfortunate places. And the bugs are biting. My brother is shooting the photo from the bridge. Four pasty white asses gleaming in the sun, water up to mid-thigh. Pretty good asses, actually, for a bunch of forty-somethings, it will later be noted by the few women who actually get to see this classic photo. I don't think we will ever do this again.

––––––––

I am standing in the river, and a twelve-inch trout just snapped off my fly. This has been the hot fly of the day. I had just caught three smaller trout on this fly, and I tie on another one of the exact same fly, the second of three in my box. After many years, I have a three-fly rule that I always try to abide by.

Experience shows that when I have a hot fly and lose it, I want to have at least two more in my box, so I am not so nervous about losing the second one. One time I tied on my only remaining matching fly, then immediately lost that one in the bushes behind me. And there I was, with no more of the same fly. I tried a few slightly larger, slightly smaller, and the same pattern in a different color. Nothing else worked like that hot fly. That is when I came up with my three-fly rule. I never wanted to be in that situation again: fish waiting and me with nothing proper to offer.

––––––––

I am standing in the river with my fourteen-year-old son, Garrett (known to the world as Bubba), who is fishing with me. I had to bring him along on this trip because he needs to be at a USA Hockey regional camp in Burlington, Vermont, on Sunday. Cheryl is at her twenty-fifth college reunion in Hanover for the weekend. So Bubba agreed to join me on my weekend with The Boys of the Grant, and I will drive him directly to his camp from here.

Before our arrival, I was a little worried that my buddies would be unable to resist telling inappropriate stories from our rugby and fraternity days in front of him, especially after a couple of beers. That hasn't been too much of a problem, fortunately. He is enjoying a different side of his old man, relaxing away from home. But the more immediate issue was this: "Dad, what do you guys have to drink other than beer?"

Oops. "Um, we have plenty of water, dude," I replied. But we have no lemonade or Gatorade or even much milk. There's just enough for coffee. Oh well, he'll survive.

Bubba and I are fishing one of my favorite pools in the Swift. It has three different inlets, two main currents near each bank and a small waterfall in the middle. The pool is deep enough in the middle to hold bigger trout, and the tail of the pool is also fairly productive.

Bubba's casting is improving, and he floats a Hornberg nicely in the current, then retrieves it wet just beneath the surface over the deeper rock crevasses. On about the tenth cast, he hooks a six-inch trout, panics for a bit, and manages to land it with the help of my net. Flush with success, he decides to try the tail of the pool on his own without his dad giving him endless advice.

As Bubba casts from a rock about thirty feet to my left, I roll cast an Elk Hair Caddis to the base of the little waterfall. Bang! A seven-inch trout. I switch to my other rod, which is rigged with sinking line, and drop a Wood Special into the current in the deeper water. I count a few seconds to let the line sink with the fly. Just as I start my retrieve—bang again! Another trout, this one about ten inches. On the next three casts, I pull out three more splendid trout.

Bubba is looking upstream at me with his mouth open. He has never really watched me fish before. "Jeeeez-us, Dad!" A grin sneaks up from my chin to my cheekbones. "I make this look easy, don't I, son?" It is pretty darned hard for a dad to impress his hotshot teenage son. I can't stop smiling.

———

I am standing in the river amazed that we didn't lose the canoe and everything in it. I am perched precariously on a piece of granite ledge, holding the stern of the canoe in one hand, trying to keep my balance while I guide the canoe to the bank. The canoe is filled with water, the result of our swamping it as we crashed over the three standing waves here at Sid Hayward Ledge. We had canoed this river several times before, but never with this much water. When we rounded the bend and saw the standing waves, we had no time to do anything but ride it out as best we could.

On the first wave, the canoe came down hard and filled about halfway. Crashing down from the second wave, it filled to about three-quarters full. On the third wave, it filled completely and began to disappear from under our asses. Billy fell or jumped out and somehow thrashed about ten feet to shore in his waders, which had quickly filled with water. As the canoe sank underneath me, I stuck my feet forward hoping to stand up, and felt the ledge beneath my feet at the same moment the tip of the stern passed through my legs. I stood up on the ledge, leaning back into the current, and grabbed the wooden handle in the stern of the canoe. And here I am, standing in the river.

I hold the canoe against the current and guide it to the nearest shore, where Billy has climbed up the bank into the alders. We realize that we somehow managed to save the canoe without losing anything but a single seat cushion.

Billy starts shivering violently from the cold water and cool evening air. I am chilled too, but for now, adrenalin is keeping me warm. "Let's get back in and start paddling, Billy. We will warm up quickly." Billy is skeptical, but realizes we don't have much choice. We are on the opposite side of the river from the road, about two miles from the take out. We have to cross somehow.

We climb back in and start paddling, feeling pretty lucky our mishap wasn't far worse. After about 200 yards, we see the next ledge and two more standing waves. "Good thing there are only two!" I say with all confidence I can muster.

———

I'm standing in the river presenting my fly carefully, cast after cast. I start thinking about how many hours over my lifetime I may have spent standing in a river. When people ask me about fishing, I am fairly quick to tell them that, while I like all kinds of fishing, I am primarily a stream fisherman. Standing in a river is my favorite place to be.

I also start to wonder whether, after thirty-five years of fishing, I have spent more time presenting flies to fish than I have spent making presentations to people at work. I'm hoping that I've spent much more time standing in a river. It may be cliché, but it's true: a bad day fishing is better than a good day at work.

———

I'm standing in the river near The Confluence gazing not at the water but up to the Diamond Peaks.

Moments ago, as I emerged from the path through the woods, I was startled by a dark shape speeding through my peripheral vision over my right shoulder. Perhaps the bald eagle had been as surprised as I to encounter another large creature on the edge of the still trees.

With a few flaps of its broad wings, it had soon gained a thousand feet and is now gracefully figure-eighting around the peaks with unimaginable grace. I'll watch as long as I can before putting a line in the water.

———

I am standing in the river, glad to be standing at all. For the last two months, I have had a back problem, a lumbar disc pinching a nerve that makes it painful to stand. My left leg and foot are weak and stupid. I have been on painkillers and just had a Cortisone shot three days ago. Sitting is fine. Walking and standing, not so good.

I love the Grant, and I love The Boys, so I came up here knowing I might not be able to fish at all. For the past day and a half, I have been sitting in the cabin, or near the river in my chair-in-a-bag, while the rest of The Boys have been fishing. I brought my camera and a book and my watercolors, so I can keep myself happy soaking in the sights and smells of the spruce and fir forest, listening to the rushing waters. I stink at watercolors but it is enough to absorb me for a while.

Today, thanks to a fairly decent night's sleep, I am feeling a bit better, and I have ridden with Bob and Ed up to the Pool of No Luck. Bob wanders upstream to the run above the pool, while Ed makes some casts at the head of the pool. A few minutes later Ed and I hear a whoop from Bob. He has caught his first fish of the day. So I decide to put on my waders and give it a try.

I walk stiffly along the bank of the Pool of No Luck and up to the glide above. Bob is casting at the top of the glide, which is about thirty yards long. I decide to try the far side near the middle. As I cast, I see a small splashy rise in the foam line. The fish are actively rising for the first time since the big rain earlier this week. Two more casts, a good drift, and I hook a small trout, about five or six inches. It flops wildly as I bring it in and pull the small hook from its mouth, before releasing it to dash back across the river.

I am thrilled that I caught a fish. It's way more than I had expected for this trip. I make a few more casts before my back tells me to go sit down. As I return to the chair near the car, Bob catches another. I get to the car, take off my waders, crack a beer, and sit back down in my chair, completely content, if a little sore. I'll be back to fish again another day.

Guy set his alarm for 4 a.m. to capture the full moon setting over the Swift Diamond at Sam's Lookout.

Meet The Boys of the Grant

The Boys enjoy banter and b.s. after dinner in Sam's Cabin. Photo by Phil Odence.

David A. Van Wie

"Guy (pronounced *ghee*), DVW"

Hometown: Troy, New York
Current home: New Gloucester, Maine
Wife: Cheryl Bascomb (Dartmouth Class of '82)
Children: Rosa (Dartmouth Class of '12), Garrett ("Bubba")
Fly-fishing experience: Started in Wyoming in 1980. 30 years in Maine and New Hampshire with a few exotic excursions.
Profession: Environmental consultant. Served a term in the Maine House of Representatives.
Other interests: Photography, bicycling, guitar, winter sports.
College connections: Roomed with Phil. Heorot fraternity with Phil and Klingon. Rugby with Phil, Klingon, and Ed. Grad school with Bob.

L. Philip Odence

"Phil, Philip, PhilO"

Hometown: Moorestown, New Jersey
Current home: Cotuit and Waltham, Massachusetts
Wife: Beth Jane Tanner Odence
Children: Clarissa ("Bookie"), Charlotte
Fly-fishing experience: Mostly at the Grant.
Profession: Technology company executive.
Other interests: Sailing, reading, barefoot running, watercolors, hiking, travel, cartoons of Young Conway.
College connections: Roomed with Norm and later Guy. Traveled with Billy. Heorot fraternity with Guy and Klingon. Rugby with Guy, Klingon, and Ed. Grad school with Bob.

Norman B. Richter

"Nerm"

Hometown: New York, New York
Current home: Glencoe, Illinois (though headed back to New England)
Wife: Pam
Children: Clara, Annika
Fly-fishing experience: None prior to the Grant, then fly-fishing for stripers on Block Island.
Profession: Tax attorney and corporate executive
Other interests: Karate, writing fiction.
College connections: Freshman roommate with Phil on same hallway with Guy. AXA with Billy.

Robert Chamberlin

"Bob"

Hometown: Western Springs, Illinois
Current home: Burlington, Vermont
Wife: Good question.
Children: Tim, Libby
Fly-fishing experience: Member of Lake Mitchell Trout Club, Vermont.
Profession: Transportation planning engineer.
Other interests: Watercolors, baseball, dogs, girls.
College connections: Thayer School of Engineering (graduate school)
with Phil and Guy.

Edwin R. Baldrige III

"Ed"

Hometown: Allentown, Pennsylvania
Current home: Kutztown, Pennsylvania
Wife: Lydia Panas
Children: Lukas, Ana, Liam
Fly-fishing experience: Many years fishing in Pennsylvania, out West, and abroad; also fishes Tenkara method.
Profession: Investment advisor.
Other interests: Travel, skiing.
College connections: Rugby with Phil, Guy, and Norm.

David H. Klinges, Jr.

"Klingon"

Hometown: Bethlehem, Pennsylvania
Current home: Princeton and Barnegat Light, New Jersey
Wife: Dana Burroughs Klinges (Dartmouth Class of '82)
Children: Grace, David (Dartmouth Class of '17)
Fly-fishing experience: None prior to the Grant.
Profession: Investment banking/project finance.
Other interests: Yankees baseball, rugby, *Sports Illustrated*.
College connections: Rugby with Guy, Ed and Phil. Heorot fraternity with Guy and Phil.

William B. Conway, Jr.

"Billy, Young Conway"

Hometown: New Orleans, Louisiana
Current home: Potomac, Maryland
Wife: Diana Edensword Conway
Children: Will, Catherine (Dartmouth Class of '17), Alexandra ('20)
Fly-fishing experience: Fishing for stripers on Martha's Vineyard.
Profession: Energy attorney.
Other interests: Beekeeping, gardening, reading, earth moving equipment.
College connections: Friends with Norm, Phil, and Guy since freshman year. Traveled with Phil. AXA fraternity with Norm. Star of Young Conway comics.

THE WITCH OF COOS
By Robert Frost

I STAID the night for shelter at a farm
Behind the mountain, with a mother and son,
Two old-believers. They did all the talking.

The Mother
Folks think a witch who has familiar spirits
She *could* call up to pass a winter evening,
But *won't*, should be burned at the stake or something.
Summoning spirits isn't "Button, button,
Who's got the button," you're to understand.
The Son
Mother can make a common table rear
And kick with two legs like an army mule.
The Mother
And when I've done it, what good have I done?
Rather than tip a table for you, let me
Tell you what Ralle the Sioux Control once told me.
He said the dead had souls, but when I asked him
How that could be—I thought the dead were souls,
He broke my trance. Don't that make you suspicious
That there's something the dead are keeping back?
Yes, there's something the dead are keeping back.
The Son
You wouldn't want to tell him what we have
Up attic, mother?
The Mother
              Bones—a skeleton.
The Son
But the headboard of mother's bed is pushed
Against the attic door: the door is nailed.
It's harmless. Mother hears it in the night
Halting perplexed behind the barrier
Of door and headboard. Where it wants to get
Is back into the cellar where it came from.
The Mother
We'll never let them, will we, son? We'll never!
The Son
It left the cellar forty years ago
And carried itself like a pile of dishes
Up one flight from the cellar to the kitchen,

Another from the kitchen to the bedroom,
Another from the bedroom to the attic,
Right past both father and mother, and neither stopped
        it.
Father had gone upstairs; mother was downstairs.
I was a baby: I don't know where I was.

The Mother

The only fault my husband found with me—
I went to sleep before I went to bed,
Especially in winter when the bed
Might just as well be ice and the clothes snow.
The night the bones came up the cellar-stairs
Toffile had gone to bed alone and left me,
But left an open door to cool the room off
So as to sort of turn me out of it.
I was just coming to myself enough
To wonder where the cold was coming from,
When I heard Toffile upstairs in the bedroom
And thought I heard him downstairs in the cellar.
The board we had laid down to walk dry-shod on
When there was water in the cellar in spring
Struck the hard cellar bottom. And then someone
Began the stairs, two footsteps for each step,
The way a man with one leg and a crutch,
Or little child, comes up. It wasn't Toffile:
It wasn't anyone who could be there.
The bulkhead double-doors were double-locked
And swollen tight and buried under snow.
The cellar windows were banked up with sawdust
And swollen tight and buried under snow.
It was the bones. I knew them—and good reason.
My first impulse was to get to the knob
And hold the door. But the bones didn't try
The door; they halted helpless on the landing,
Waiting for things to happen in their favor.
The faintest restless rustling ran all through them.
I never could have done the thing I did
If the wish hadn't been too strong in me
To see how they were mounted for this walk.
I had a vision of them put together
Not like a man, but like a chandelier.
So suddenly I flung the door wide on him.
A moment he stood balancing with emotion,

And all but lost himself. (A tongue of fire
Flashed out and licked along his upper teeth.
Smoke rolled inside the sockets of his eyes.)
Then he came at me with one hand outstretched,
The way he did in life once; but this time
I struck the hand off brittle on the floor,
And fell back from him on the floor myself.
The finger-pieces slid in all directions.
(Where did I see one of those pieces lately?
Hand me my button-box—it must be there.)

I sat up on the floor and shouted, "Toffile,
It's coming up to you." It had its choice
Of the door to the cellar or the hall.
It took the hall door for the novelty,
And set off briskly for so slow a thing,
Still going every which way in the joints, though,
So that it looked like lightning or a scribble,
From the slap I had just now given its hand.

I listened till it almost climbed the stairs
From the hall to the only finished bedroom,
Before I got up to do anything;
Then ran and shouted, "Shut the bedroom door,
Toffile, for my sake!" "Company," he said,
"Don't make me get up; I'm too warm in bed."
So lying forward weakly on the handrail
I pushed myself upstairs, and in the light
(The kitchen had been dark) I had to own
I could see nothing. "Toffile, I don't see it.
It's with us in the room, though. It's the bones."
"What bones?" "The cellar bones—out of the grave."

That made him throw his bare legs out of bed
And sit up by me and take hold of me.
I wanted to put out the light and see
If I could see it, or else mow the room,
With our arms at the level of our knees,
And bring the chalk-pile down. "I'll tell you what—
It's looking for another door to try.
The uncommonly deep snow has made him think
Of his old song, *The Wild Colonial Boy,*
He always used to sing along the tote-road.

He's after an open door to get out-doors.
Let's trap him with an open door up attic."
Toffile agreed to that, and sure enough,
Almost the moment he was given an opening,
The steps began to climb the attic stairs.
I heard them. Toffile didn't seem to hear them.
"Quick!" I slammed to the door and held the knob.
"Toffile, get nails." I made him nail the door shut,
And push the headboard of the bed against it.

Then we asked was there anything
Up attic that we'd ever want again.
The attic was less to us than the cellar.
If the bones liked the attic, let them like it,
Let them *stay* in the attic. When they sometimes
Come down the stairs at night and stand perplexed
Behind the door and headboard of the bed,
Brushing their chalky skull with chalky fingers,
With sounds like the dry rattling of a shutter,
That's what I sit up in the dark to say—
To no one any more since Toffile died.
Let them stay in the attic since they went there.
I promised Toffile to be cruel to them
For helping them be cruel once to him.
The Son
    We think they had a grave down in the cellar.
The Mother
    We know they had a grave down in the cellar.
The Son
    We never could find out whose bones they were.
The Mother
    Yes, we could too, son. Tell the truth for once.
    They were a man's his father killed for me.
    I mean a man he killed instead of me.
    The least I could do was help dig their grave.
    We were about it one night in the ce'lar.
    Son knows the story: but 'twas not for him
    To tell the truth, suppose the time had come.
    Son looks surprised to see me end a lie
    We'd kept up all these years between ourselves
    So as to have it ready for outsiders.
    But tonight I don't care enough to lie—
    I don't remember why I ever cared.

Toffile, if he were here, I don't believe
Could tell you why he ever cared himself. . . .

She hadn't found the finger-bone she wanted
Among the buttons poured out in her lap.

I verified the name next morning: Toffile.
The rural letter-box said Toffile Barre.

Robert Frost

From *Poetry - A Magazine of Verse,* Vol. XIX No. IV, January 1922

References & Sources

The following website, articles, and materials contain information about the Second College Grant, some of which was used for reference in writing this book.

Hunting & Fishing At The Second Dartmouth College Grant, 2012. Brochure from Dartmouth Outdoor Programs.

Catch and Release Fishing, National Park Services, National Resources Program (Water Resources Division)

Wintering With Amasa Ward, 1889-1890. Jack Noon, Moose Country Press, 2009.

"Two Centuries of Timber and Trampers: Where Recreation and Logging Coexist." Chuck Wooster. *Northern Woodlands Magazine,* Summer 2006:22-27.

"Northern Exposure." Photographs by Paul Rezendes. *Dartmouth Alumni Magazine,* May/June 2001:28-39.

"Mysteries of the Hand on the Rock." John Harrigan, *North Country Notebook,* May 22-29, 2002.

"A Life in the Wild." Nelson Bryant '46. *Dartmouth Alumni Magazine,* May/June 2001:40-41.

"Mr. Smith Meets the President." Edmund Ware Smith, *Sports Illustrated,* August 29, 1955. http://www.si.com/vault/1955/08/29/604960/mr-smith-meets-the-president

"Special College Grant Issue," *Woodsmoke.* October, 1970.

"Sam Brungot Retires." *Dartmouth Alumni Magazine,* 1962.

"Brief History of the Grant." Bennett, November 1952.

"Trees Provide Dartmouth Scholarships." *NY Lumber Trade Journal,* December 1940.

"The College Grant." Dr. John M. Gile, *Dartmouth Alumni Magazine,* March 1922.

"Notice to Lumbermen." May 1, 1888.

History of Coos County, Georgia Drew Merrill, W.A. Fergusson, Syracuse, N.Y., 1888

Various papers from Dartmouth's Rauner Special Collections Library, including papers and correspondence of President John Sloan Dickey.

Web page: http://www.dartmouth.edu/~finance/departments/secondgrant/grantarticles.html